The Transformations of Allegory

CONCEPTS OF LITERATURE

GENERAL EDITOR : WILLIAM RIGHTER

Department of English
University of Warwick

Volumes in this series include

COMPARATIVE LITERATURE
Henry Gifford,   *University of Bristol*

STYLE AND STYLISTICS
Graham Hough,   *University of Cambridge*

LITERATURE AND DRAMA
Stanley Wells,   *The Shakespeare Institute, Stratford-upon-Avon*

ON REALISM
J. P. Stern,   *University College, London*

The Transformations of Allegory

Gay Clifford

Department of English
University of Warwick

LONDON AND BOSTON
ROUTLEDGE & KEGAN PAUL

First published in 1974
by Routledge & Kegan Paul Ltd
Broadway House, 68-74 Carter Lane,
London EC4V 5EL and
9 Park Street,
Boston, Mass. 02108, USA
Set in Linotype Pilgrim
and printed in Great Britain by
Northumberland Press Limited
Gateshead

ISBN 0 7100 7976 1 (c)
      0 7100 7977 X (p)
Library of Congress Catalog Card No. 74-84170

General editor's introduction

The study of literature has normally centred on the consideration of work, author, or historical period. But increasingly there is a demand for a more analytic approach, for investigation and explanation of literary concepts of crucial ideas and issues—topics which are of general importance to the critical consideration of particular works. This series undertakes to provide a clear description and critical evaluation of such important ideas as 'symbolism', 'realism', 'style' and other terms used in literary discussion. It also undertakes to define the relationship of literature to other intellectual disciplines: anthropology, philosophy, psychology, etc., for it is in connection with such related fields that much important recent critical work has been done. *Concepts of Literature* will both account for the methodology of literary study, and will define its dimensions by reference to the many activities that throw light upon it. Individual works will describe the fundamental outlines of particular problems and explore the frontiers that they suggest. The series as a whole will provide a survey of recent literary thought.

Much discussion of allegory is concerned to isolate the special characteristics of the mode, suggesting a form of narrative set apart and committed to its expository and didactic purposes. While agreeing on its ideal and non-mimetic features, Gay Clifford is concerned with its inner flexibility, with the power of allegorical forms to undergo a complex evolution and multiple transformations. So to her the concept of allegory is not rigid and self-contained but complex and many-sided, not bound to a narrow historical context but capable of adapting to many. Certain traditional features of its narrative may persist: the formal patterns of conflict and opposition, or the structured use of analogy. But these are subject both to formal mutations and to changes of coloration that come from various historical epochs. It is this innate adaptability that has permitted the conservative, affirmative voice of a collective moral world to convey the sceptical, subversive, isolated innerness of *The Castle*, or the traditional vehicle of didacticism to express the articulation of doubt. So allegory is not only a means of formalizing a stable universe; that is only one of its incarnations. It is also the 'figuring forth' of an historical movement from ordered to uncertain, from theocentric to anthropocentric, reflecting in turn the advent of puritanism, the development of science, the rise of capitalism, and a continually refined psychological exploration of man's inner life.

Contents

Author's note

Translations in the text are my own, except where an alternative is specified in the reference.

1
The concept

> Then I began to dream a marvellous dream, that I was in a
> wilderness I knew not where. As I looked into the east and
> high against the sun I saw a tower on a hillock, excellently
> made; a deep valley beneath a dungeon therein, with deep
> ditches and dark and terrifying to behold. Between the two I
> discovered a fair plain full of people, all manner of men, the
> poor and the rich, working and wandering about as the world
> demands.

This is part of the beginning of Langland's poem *Piers Plowman*,
written towards the end of the 1370s. It is a dream, but not necessarily more dreamlike than the description with which *The Faerie
Queene* opens:

> A gentle knight was pricking on the plaine,
>   Y cladd in mightie armes and siluer shielde, ...
> But on his brest a bloudie Crosse he bore,
>   The deare remembrance of his dying Lord, ...
> Vpon a great aduenture he was bond,
>   That greatest *Gloriana* to him gaue,
>   That greatest Glorious Queene of *Faerie* lond, ...
> A louely Ladie rode him faire beside,
>   Vpon a lowly Asse more white then snow,
>   Yet she much whiter, ...
> And by her in a line a milke white lambe she lad.

Spenser concentrates on people rather than on places, as is usual
in the tradition of chivalric Romance, but like Langland he suggests

the symbolic or emblematic nature of his subject. Bunyan's *The Pilgrim's Progress* begins: 'As I walk'd through the wilderness of this world, I lighted on a certain place, where was a Denn; And I laid me down in that place to sleep: And as I slept I dreamed a Dream.' Here the wilderness and the dungeon are in the world while the dream starts with family life, neighbours, and conversation. These are soon abandoned for places and experiences that are unreal and enigmatic even though the comparative realism of a conversation between two people provides the impetus. Christian laments his burden of guilt to Evangelist:

> Then said *Evangelist*, If this be thy condition, why standest thou still? He answered, Because I know not whither to go. Then he gave him a *Parchment-Roll*, and there was written within, *Fly from the wrath to come.*
>
> The Man, therefore Read it, and looking upon *Evangelist* very carefully; said, Whither must I fly? Then said *Evangelist*, pointing with his finger over a very wide Field, Do you see yonder *Wicket-gate*? The Man said, No. Then said the other, Do you see yonder shining light? He said, I think I do. Then said *Evangelist* keep that light in your eye, and go up directly thereto; so shalt thou see the Gate; at which, when thou knockest, it shall be told thee what thou shalt do.
>
> So I saw in my Dream that the Man began to run. Now, he had not run far from his own door, but his Wife and Children perceiving it, began to cry after him to return: but the Man put his fingers in his Ears, and ran on crying, Life, Life, Eternal Life: so he looked not behind him, but fled towards the middle of the Plain.

Each of these passages confronts us with a strange world, which though distinctive resembles the others in its combination of elusiveness and familiarity. Their strangeness derives not from exoticism, but from the fact that they are so neutral, so indefinite, and yet immediately suggest that they mean something important. 'A wilderness', 'a tower', 'a great adventure', 'a very wide field' — the language is not particularly elaborate or rhetorical or even poetic, but it conveys urgency and even mystery. Part of the urgency comes from the neutrality of the vocabulary and from the paratactic structure: we accept that these things are familiar in some way, even while we sense that they are also remote and dangerous. We are compelled to read on in order to understand this enigmatic lack of congruity. The worlds of allegory are only half-familiar and they are rarely safe. Neither protagonists nor readers can predict with any security what phenomena they will encounter or precisely what these phenomena will signify. We have to immerse ourselves in the world of each allegory until we discover its peculiar and persuasive internal logic.

By contrast, the much-quoted opening sentence of *Emma* offers us principally the pleasures of recognition :

> Emma Woodhouse, handsome, clever, and rich, with a
> comfortable home and happy disposition, seemed to unite
> some of the best blessings of existence; and had lived
> nearly twenty-one years in the world with very little to
> distress or vex her.

We read on to find out what happens, rather than to find out what this means, or how the meaning might be applied to our own existence. This rather simple-minded distinction has been made at the outset because I believe that people sometimes still try to enter allegorical worlds in the way they might that of Hartfield and Highbury.

Emma and the greater part of nineteenth- and twentieth-century fiction is accessible in a way that allegory is not, and readers have come to expect accessibility from imaginative literature. In consequence the comparative inaccessibility of allegory poses special problems both for readers and critics. I have used quotation at some length so that three great allegories might begin to effect their own demonstration before argument intervened between them and the reader. Much of the rhetoric of this book is aimed at persuading readers of the particular power of allegory, its imaginative and intellectual – and moral – pleasures. It in part attempts to reinstate this kind of literature as well as to describe it. This implies no disrespect to the many critics who have written sensitively about allegory in the past few decades, since their writing has contributed to my own enthusiasm. But while they and the allegories themselves are good advocates for the mode, it is still somehow unfashionable.

This unfashionableness is a legacy of much Romantic and post-Romantic criticism, in which the didacticism and intellectuality of allegory are seen as crude and wilful limitations upon emotional and archetypal significance. Yeats equates the allegorist with the pedant in his essay 'The Symbolism of Poetry'; he suggests in writing of Spenser that allegory was not 'natural at all' to him, and that the allegory

> disappoints and interrupts our preoccupation with the beautiful and sensuous life he has called up before our eyes. It interrupts us most when he copies Langland, and writes in what he believes to be a mood of edification, and the least when he is not quite serious, when he sets before us some procession like a Court pageant made to celebrate a wedding or a crowning. One cannot think that he should have occupied himself with moral and religious questions at all.
>
> *(Selected Criticism*, ed. Jeffares, p.110)

This seems to me unjust, untrue, and pernicious. In *The Faerie Queene* the seriousness is a part of beauty. How can we accept that Calidore's vision (VI X 11) of the poet piping for

> An hundred naked maidens lilly white,
> All raunged in a ring, and dauncing in delight.

is 'not quite serious'? The 'beautiful and sensuous' *is* the edification.
　Many of the criticisms of allegory made by post-Romantic critics like Yeats are the product of a particular conception of the function (and psychology) of literature. They tend to judge allegory in competition with symbolism and as a result misunderstand many of its features and, more seriously, deny the effects which it can achieve.

> Allegory, and, to a much greater degree, symbolism are a natural language by which the soul when entranced, or even in ordinary sleep, communes with God and with angels. They can speak of things which cannot be spoken of in any other language.
>
> (Yeats, *op. cit.* p.109)

But allegory is also a natural language for visionary strangeness and intensity, and its moral and intellectual preoccupations strengthen rather than diminish this visionary power.
　Most readers will readily acknowledge the existence of allegory

as a literary form during the Middle Ages and the Renaissance, but few of them will concede its power to survive beyond those periods. Some even deny any importance or vitality to those later works which suggest its continuance. Conversely, some other critics, the most distinguished of whom is Angus Fletcher, see it as omnipresent: far from being as limited in time as the sonnet sequence or the mystery play, it is a 'symbolic mode' apparent in varying degrees not only in literary works of all periods but in all art forms and media. One of the more unfortunate consequences of this extended meaning of the term is that 'allegorical' is applied in the most vague and impressionistic ways, particularly to modern works. Professor Fletcher cannot himself be held responsible for the loose employment of the term, since his work on allegory (1964) is scrupulous in its definitions and highly discriminating. His book constitutes the most valuably comprehensive study of the subject; it would be impossible to disregard it however much one might disagree with some of the criteria by which he defines allegory.

A compromise between these extremes seems desirable for two reasons. First, a number of works written after the Middle Ages and the Renaissance – the 'classic' periods for allegory – cannot be categorized or, more importantly, understood without employing the concept. This suggests that it is not possible to delimit allegory historically; at the least, it seems unnecessary to deprive ourselves of a term which is still demonstrably the most appropriate for a certain kind of writing. Second, both 'classic' allegories and modern, or more modern, ones share features which clearly differentiate them from other contemporaneous fiction forms. It is possible to claim that allegory may take many forms, without weakening the definition to the point of saying it can take *any* form.

Certain features of allegory could be seen as generic; the extended and extensive use of personification and personified abstractions and, especially, the incorporation of commentary and interpretation into the action. But essentially allegory is, like irony, a mode, and capable of subsuming many different genres and forms. There is comic allegory in *Gulliver's Travels* and *A Tale of a Tub*, tragic (and Gothic) allegory in *Frankenstein*, allegorical chivalric Romance in *The Faerie Queene*, satirical allegory in *Piers Plowman*, historical allegory in *Animal Farm*, an allegorical journey in *The Pilgrim's Progress*, journey combined with debate and vision in *Piers Plowman*. Unless we are to end up with a definition of allegory resembling Polonius's description of the Players' repertoire in *Hamlet* (tragical, comical, historical, and pastoral at one blow), it is necessary to create a sense of its particular identity. This can only be done cumulatively, by describing the features of a number of individual works. The difficulty here is to avoid the sort of value judgments that too often convert description into prescription. If the reader believes that Dante's *La Divina Commedia* is a better work of literature than Alain de Lille's *De Planctu Naturae* and is discussing them both as allegories, the temptation is to argue that the qualities which contribute to the 'superiority' of the former always and in all cases make for better allegory. An additional reason for resisting this temptation is that allegory serves different functions in different periods and communities. *Le Roman de la Rose* explores the experiences and difficulties of a lover in the pursuit of his erotic (and to a lesser degree social) ambitions; *Piers Plowman* those of a soul in pursuit of salvation for himself and the community. What makes one highly effective allegory and possibly also good poetry could be disastrous on both counts for the other. Our criteria for value cannot be purely formal.

Any mode that survives over a long period is likely to take on very different shapes under pressure of the needs and expectations of different generations. With allegory the transformations are more than usually extensive because its formal features are usually subordinated to didactic purpose or to the preconceived intellectual structures the author wants to convey. In the case of the novel the same epistolary form can express both the morality of *Pamela* and that of *Les Liaisons dangereuses*, but what could be called the form of allegorical Romance is radically different in *The Faerie Queene* and in *Le Roman de la Rose*. Nor is the difference altogether explicable in terms of period, since Spenser's archaism gives his narrative a considerable resemblance to both visionary and non-visionary medieval Romances. A comparison between the presentation of the Palmer in Book II of *The Faerie Queene* with that of Reason in *Le Roman de la Rose* shows that even the basic device of personification functions very differently in the two works. The Palmer is both a person and a personification, having a dramatic function as well as a polemic one: Reason is principally the exponent of one side of an argument. This is because *Le Roman de la Rose* is concerned chiefly with a particular experience (sexual love), while for Spenser's Guyon, whom the Palmer advises, sexuality is only one part of his adventures, and those adventures only one part of a much larger abstract structure concerned with the whole idea of Virtue. Reason is there to put the case for not loving, the Palmer to exemplify the kinds of counsel the good man (and, specifically, the temperate one) may rely upon both from within himself and from without.

The fact that the structure of the fiction is dominated or preceded by the ideological structure causes considerable problems to any modern reader of allegory. It tends to make the critic sound defensive, if not about the values themselves, at least of their dominant role, since it has become something of a commonplace that a writer ought to conceal moral purpose and work almost subliminally to persuade. The case is made more difficult by the fact that many other characteristic qualities of allegory are also unpleasing or unfamiliar to readers who have grown up on nine-teenth- and twentieth-century fiction: apart from being overtly moralistic or didactic, it is abstract, speculative, and discursive, and often expounds cosmic or political systems that are hierarchical and conservative.

Moreover, though allegory seeks to express movement and process as well as structures and is therefore essentially a narrative mode, it is very different from the more popular, generally mimetic, sorts of narrative. But, oversimply, one could say that the allegorist wants to communicate certain generalized formulations about the nature of human experience and the organization of the world, and shapes his narrative so as to reveal these gradually and per-suasively to the reader, whereas the playwright or novelist would choose his form and narrative subject matter and then allow any thematic elements to emerge from it almost incidentally. One cannot imagine Bunyan saying (as Tolstoy about Anna Karenina) that Hopeful grew and developed of his own accord. In mimetic literature the reader's involvement often derives from a strong sense of both the particularity of the action and the uniqueness of the characters – the author may possibly, but not necessarily, invite the reader to see them as typical or representative or as embodying abstract statements. It would be possible, for example, to read several of the Rougon-Macquart novels before perceiving the degree of importance that the concepts of heredity and environmental conditioning held for Zola. In contrast, allegory invites its readers from the outset to see the particular narrative as being also a series of generalized statements, and demands that concepts be identified simultaneously in their fictional and ideological roles. As Northrop Frye commented, 'we have actual allegory when a poet explicitly indicates the relationship of his images to examples and precepts' (*Anatomy*, p.90).

It is of course important that the abstraction, the universal, *coexists* with its particular manifestation in the narrative. The view of allegory as a mere translation of non-poetic ideas into more or less poetic form (exemplified by Coleridge's comments in the *Statesman's Manual* and the 1818 lecture notes) is one that has hampered many critics. Even Hazlitt, who is often shrewdly perceptive about works remote from early Romantic tastes, is led to say some very strange things about *The Faerie Queene* by his belief that 'meaning' is secondary to the narrative fiction.

Though allegory is the most abstract and intellectual of all forms of fiction, its authors need a strong sense of the concrete and a lively visual imagination. The writer is concerned with recurrent patterns of human experience and the immaterial or metaphysical patterns of which these are supposedly a reflection, but he necessarily relies on particulars to express these abstractions and generalities. T. S. Eliot's phrase, 'direct sensuous apprehension of thought', perfectly expresses what happens in allegory, and his assertion that this integration of the sensuous and intellectual becomes impossible after the seventeenth century is very pertinent to the fortunes of allegorical writing in later periods. To write good allegory and to derive pleasure from reading it requires a taste for speculation, and only continual raids on the public world of the senses provide the terms in which speculation can be expressed. To take a minor and even naïve example, when Sir Scudamour is attacked by Care (*Faerie Queene*, Book IV) he is any man kept from rest by painful thoughts. Care is Care-itself, a personification of worries which cause insomnia, but Spenser gives dramatic form to the idea by presenting Care as a smith who tortures Scudamour physically.

> [He] A paire of redwhot yron tongs did take
> Out of the burning cinders, and therewith
> Vnder his side him nipt, that forst to wake,
> He felt his hart for very paine to quake. . . .

(IV v 44)

The basis of the metaphor here is personification, but personification is only one of the means by which ideas can be made concrete. It is poor allegory, mere allegorization, that uses it exclusively. In *Piers Plowman* the Incarnation is described in these terms:

For heuene myȝte nouȝte holden it . it was so heuy of hym-self,
Tyl it hadde of þe erthe . yeten his fylle.
And when it haued of þis folde . flesshe & blode taken,
Was neuere leef upon lynde . liȝter þer-after,
And portatyf and persant . as þe poynt of a nedle,
That myȝte non armure it lette . ne none heiȝ walles.

(I 151-6)

(For heaven might not contain it, it was so heavy in itself, until it had eaten its fill of the earth. And when it had taken flesh and blood of this world no leaf on a lime tree was lighter thereafter, and it was easy to bear and sharp as the point of a needle, so that no armour might hinder it nor any high walls.)

The subject, divine love, is not a knight or a weapon called 'Love' attacking other armed knights or a fortified town, even though direct personifications of 'Love' were a commonplace of the period at which Langland wrote. Instead, an event in Christian history and the theology of that event are expressed simultaneously; and even though it is fortuitous that in Middle English the pronouns 'it' and 'him' and 'its' and 'his' may be linguistically undifferentiated, in this context it contributes to a perfect balance between the idea of a person and a concept. C. S. Lewis said (*Allegory of Love*, pp.160-1) that the lines are 'perfectly accurate and clear in doctrine; and the result is as concrete, as fully incarnate, as if the poet were writing about apples or butter'.

This example suggests the way in which the allegorist may use all the kinds and degrees of metaphor to give concepts vitality: visual images are an important vehicle for the meaning of the protagonists' experiences. The larger images of landscape and setting and individual visual detail both reveal the local significance of an event, and also connect it to the overall significance of the narrative. A later section will deal at greater length with this aspect of allegory.

The commonplace definition of allegory as an 'extended

metaphor' is still one of the most useful. But as the comments above suggest, the need to give allegorical meaning a material form makes symbols another important component in allegory. The distinction between symbolism and allegory has always been a difficult one to formulate, but some attempt to do this may not be out of place here. As a preliminary it is necessary to differentiate between the occasional or even habitual use of symbols, and symbolism as a mode *per se*. It might be better to use the French word, *symbolisme*, since that makes the precise literary-historical significance of the term more explicit. Symbols are a component in a very wide range of literature, including allegory, but in the *symboliste* writing of the late nineteenth and early twentieth century that component forms the basis of a particular aesthetic.

In many works which are neither allegorical nor symbolist certain images possess a large-scale symbolic significance: the bubbling still of crude alcohol in *L'Assommoir*, the mounds of carefully gleaned and picked dust and rubbish in *Our Mutual Friend*, and the garden in Marvell's poem are all intense analogies for something other than themselves. Allegory, with its reliance on the visual and concrete to convey abstract and moral meaning, necessarily uses symbols in the same sort of way, though with equal emphasis on the intellectual and emotive significance of the image – whereas in Dickens, for example, the emotive aspect is usually uppermost. The authors of allegory invent objects to suggest the essentials of the concept they wish to explore. They also use established traditional symbols, particularly in earlier allegories. Christian is armed in the House Beautiful with symbolic weapons and armour such as the breastplate, All-Prayer, known to Bunyan and his readers through The Epistle to the Ephesians and the icono-graphic traditions of Christian militancy. In *The Faerie Queene* armour is only occasionally symbolic in itself, but the nature and intentions of a knight are often represented by the device on his shield. Atin, who stirs up 'strife and cruell fight' for his lord Pyrochles (a figure of Wrath), carries a shield showing

> A flaming fire in midst of bloudy field,
> And round about the wreath this word was writ,
> *Burnt I do burne.*
>
> (II iv 38)

Spenser's contemporary readers, familiar with the Renaissance use of *imprese*, would easily have interpreted such emblematic symbolism.

In later periods the traditional or conventional symbol could be counter-productive and serve only to create obscurity. As a result writers increasingly need to use commonplace images in a symbolic way: as the symbols of classical myth and the Christian Middle Ages alike become embarrassingly artificial, ordinary events and objects have to be intensified and made to carry a concentration of meaning if they are to have symbolic force. In *The Trial* legal process stands among other things for all the complex means by which bureaucratic societies thwart and obfuscate the desires and ambitions of the individual, and a comparably extensive and symbolic use of the same central image occurs in the non-allegorical *Bleak House*.

The use of symbols – objects or events or persons standing for something other and generally greater than themselves – is fundamental to allegory, but its authors need to know when to abandon it. If a sense of the concrete and visual is necessary, so also is a sense of narrative coherence. A symbol in allegory has to be susceptible to the sort of description that tells us what it means, but it should not suggest so many meanings that the dramatic continuum is shattered, for it is on this continuum that the overall sense of the allegory depends. The strength but also the limitation of symbols is that they tend to be static, with all the ramifications of meaning focused within the symbol. In allegory the concern is always with process, with the way in which various elements of an imaginative or intellectual system interact, and with the effects of this system or structure on and within individuals. To express change and process allegorical action often takes the form of a journey, a quest, or a pursuit: this becomes the metaphor by which a process of learning for both protagonists and readers is expressed. In the course of their adventures the heroes of allegory discover which ideals are worth pursuing and what things are obstacles to that pursuit. The narrative action thus gradually establishes a hierarchy of value and dis-value. It also provides a means for expressing – via dramatic relationships and imagery, for example – a complex pattern of connections between various ideas and abstractions. Allegories have an immense diversity of objectives, salvation in *Piers Plowman*, true courtesy in Book VI of *The Faerie Queene*, sexual possession and pleasure in *Le Roman de la Rose*,

K.'s attempts to establish his identity and gain access to the Castellan in *The Castle*. But all of them are concerned with the way in which the characters go about achieving these objectives as much as with actual attainment, the conclusion of the narrative. It is this process which symbols on their own cannot express, for symbols are primarily static and allegory is kinetic. One might say that in *The Trial* and *The Castle* the Law and the Castellan are symbols, while K.'s involvement in the process of law and his attempt to reach the Castellan are allegories. The kinesis of an allegory, its narrative movement, is directed by the major objective and by the author's desire that readers should perceive what the objective is. This limits the symbolic meaning that any object or event may have.

In *symboliste* writing the conventions of established traditional symbols are often rejected or used parodically, and the various symbols unconnected by narrative or by systematic organization into any sort of moral hierarchy independent of the reader. Allegory cannot be quite so random, even though it may be arbitrary to the extent of having symbols chosen and assigned meaning at the author's discretion. Ultimately, the meanings must refer back to the overall purpose and certainly not conflict with it. Certainly, the desire to express forward narrative movement within the symbolist mode has exercised many major poets, notably Yeats in his attempt to write a symbolist drama, but it is arguable that this is working against the grain of a mode in which the best effects are often achieved by fragmentation and dissolution. In a symbolist poem the poet is free to designate anything in the world or his imagination as a symbol: as Gide put it in the 'Traité du Narcisse' (part of the *Théorie du Symbole*), 'A-t-on compris que j'appelle *symbole* tout ce qui parait?' And when the choice is made, no limitations of meaning need necessarily be imposed. In Yeats's 'The Tower' he bequeaths his pride to 'upstanding man' and goes on to elaborate the concept as follows:

> Pride, like that of the morn,
> When the headlong light is loose,
> Or that of the fabulous horn,
> Or that of the sudden shower
> When all streams are dry,
> Or that of the hour

When the swan must fix his eye
Upon a fading gleam,
Float out upon a long
Last reach of glittering stream
And there sing his last song.

There is a marked contrast here between the specificity of the definite articles which introduce the second term of each simile, and the vague suggestiveness of the passage as a whole. Such contrasts are characteristic of symbolist poetry. The reader's response to 'his last song' will be richer if he remembers *Le Chanson de Roland* and the hero's refusal to blow his horn to summon aid to Roncevaux, or associates 'the fabulous horn' with one of those in Celtic and Arthurian myth. But the effectiveness of the poem does not absolutely depend on such interpretation or on knowledge of traditional sources. The associations are deliberately fragmented, 'pride, like that..., or that..., or that...', and expressed through nouns rather than verbs. In Langland's account of the Incarnation quoted above (p.9) divine love may not be personified, but it is the subject or object of six verbs in as many lines, and there is a definite narrative sequence from one verb to the next.

The 'heap of broken images' in *The Waste Land*, dead tree, red rock, the thunder, dead mountain, the Tarot pack, may suggest 'the present decay of eastern Europe' (T. S. Eliot's phrase in the notes) but it also suggests a multitude of other things. Images and symbols are deliberately separated from their contexts and subsequently re-assembled so that they work cumulatively or by friction on one another. This technique, used here by T. S. Eliot in an extreme form, appears in many other twentieth-century art forms such as the cinema (and now seems such a commonplace that one suspects some artists of aiming at a fragmented lack of coherence for its own sake or to create a portentous effect). It is quite different from the techniques of allegory, and produces quite different effects. The reader may well be irritated by apparent irrelevancy in *Piers Plowman*, *The Trial*, or *The Faerie Queene* (though less in the latter because there the narrative impulse is as strong as any dreamlike or visionary one). But the breaks in the action are caused by the irruption of something which refers back to the general direction of the work or to some central system. In certain modern allegories, like Kafka's two major works, the arbitrary and often obscure nature of the action, the suggestion that only the hero (like the reader of a symbolist poem) can assign meaning to his experiences, of course suggest affinities with symbolist literature. It is not altogether surprising that contemporaneous works in two different modes should reflect similar literary tastes and intellectual preoccupations. But symbolism is still fundamentally different from allegory which is distinguished by its reliance on structured narrative. It would be ridiculous to say that symbolism is impossible without narrative: of allegory it would be true.

C. S. Lewis said in *The Allegory of Love* that 'Symbolism is a mode of thought, but allegory is a mode of expression' (p.48). While this observation is a preliminary to several pages of acute and illuminating analysis it needs some modification – though in making any modifications it must in fairness be remembered that this influential formulation was specifically directed at clearing medieval allegory of the charge of being 'mystical' and mysterious, and that Lewis was not concerned with any allegories later than *The Faerie Queene*. Certainly we need to acknowledge that allegory is 'a mode of expression' in the sense that it is primarily a literary mode. But it is also a mode of thought in that it represents a way of thinking about literature and the function of literature, and of thinking about the world. The author of allegory believes in pattern, he believes that it is valid to talk about human experience in terms of repetition and generalization, and he assumes that his readers will understand his narrative, not just as the record of a unique human experience (whether Dante's journey through hell to heaven, or K.'s through the exhausting ramifications of the Law, or Calidore's through the world of pastoral) but as an expression of larger kinds of truth.

2 Narrative forms: the kinesis of allegory

Kinetic energy is defined in the OED as 'the power of doing work possessed by a moving body by virtue of its motion', and kinetics as 'the branch of dynamics which investigates the relations between the motions of bodies and the forces acting upon them; opposed to *Statics*, which treats of bodies in equilibrium'. The business of the maker and critic of allegory is exactly such an investigation seen in philosophic, moral, and imaginative terms. The fundamental narrative forms of allegory are the journey, battle or conflict, the quest or search, and transformation: i.e. some form of controlled or directed process. The control is provided by the object of the journey, combat, or quest: we interpret the significance of the 'motion' of the characters and of the forces affecting them in the light of knowledge about the direction in which they travel. Thus in *Le Roman de la Rose* we know the Lover is a lover because he swears allegiance to the God of Love, and because his energies are entirely devoted to the courtship of the Rose. In his dialogues with Reason, whatever the absolute truth of her hard-headed warnings against enslavement to love, we know that she represents only a temporary disincentive to his pursuit. She cannot divert the course of the action without the Lover ceasing to be a lover, and the allegory ceasing to be an allegory of love. Of course, if Reason were to appear in a sacred or spiritual allegory her role would be more influential, and we would be prepared for this by awareness of a qualitatively different objective for the allegorical action. R. W. Frank (1953) argued that in reading medieval personification allegories the names of characters are important in determining the significance of an encounter. This is true of this particular kind of allegory, but with the mode in general at least as important a guide to meaning is provided by the objectives of the action – both the internal objectives, the aims of the characters, towards the fulfilment of which the narrative moves, and the external objectives, the didactic purpose of the author.

The main direction of the action is usually signalled at the outset. The Dreamer hero of *Piers Plowman* asks 'How may I save my soul? How may I know the true from the false?' and these questions initiate the movement of the poem. Christian asks 'Whither must I fly?'; Spenser's knightly heroes are assigned particular tasks (the destruction of the great Dragon, or the enchantress Acrasia, or the Blatant Beast) and even where we do not at once know what that task is, other clues are provided. The cross on the breast and shield of the Redcrosse Knight, 'the deare remembrance of his dying Lord', suggests his other title, the Knight of Holiness, and he is champion and companion of Una, whose name implies the singleness of truth. His very first battle (in Book i, Canto i) is with Error who is not simply a revolting monster, but particularized by vomiting up books and papers and a brood of offspring who prey upon their mother's body as she dies. His attribute and name and that of his companion, and the nature of his antagonist, indicate that he is a religious hero, the defender of a true and unified faith.

Modern allegories differ from their predecessors in that there is no firmly established hierarchy of value to define or give meaning to the progress of the characters. In *The Trial* and *The Castle* the systems of the Law and of a provincial, almost feudal, bureaucracy both appear on the surface to be defined and limited. In fact both the locality and the significance of the action are constantly shifting, and elude any ultimate definition entailing value for either K. or the reader. The floating imagery 'becomes imbued with doubt and anxiety; hierarchy itself causes fear, hatred, tentative approach, tentative retreat. The sure sense of one's place in the sun has gone. The sure identification of the hero with governing political or cultural ideals has gone. Doubt inhibits action. Piety of any kind becomes difficult or impossible' (Fletcher, *Allegory*, p.143). But if the possibility of progress through a hierarchy of value either upwards (anagogy) or downwards (katagogy) is rejected, the notion of progress is still retained emblematically. The expectation of progress is created and then frustrated in a series of fragmented incidents.

In *The Castle* the device of the quest is inverted, as are mythological imagery and the device of the fable in *The Trial*. Soon after K. arrives in the village he sets out to reach the castle. His first glimpse of it – it was shrouded in mist and darkness when he first arrived – places it firmly as the object of a quest, almost the castle of fairy tale and Romance:

> he could see the Castle above him clearly defined in the
> glittering air, its outline made still more definite by
> the moulding of snow covering it in a thin layer.
>
> (*The Castle*, p.15)

There is heavy snow down in the village, 'making progress as laborious as on the main road the previous day'.

> But up on the hill everything soared light and free into the
> air, or at least so it appeared from down below.
>   On the whole this distant prospect of the Castle satisfied
> K.'s expectations.
>
> (*ibid.*, p.15)

The clarity and freedom of this image are things perceived from a distance, unattainables. Unlike the castles of Romance quest it neither becomes more beautiful nor more sinister, nor even does it simply disappear. It becomes ordinary and unreachable.

> It was neither an old stronghold nor a new mansion, but a rambling pile consisting of innumerable small buildings closely packed together and of one or two storeys; if K. had not known that it was a castle he might have taken it for a little town. ... The tower above him ... perhaps of the main building, was uniformly round, part of it graciously mantled with ivy, pierced by small windows that glittered in the sun, a somewhat maniacal glitter, and topped by what looked like an attic, with battlements that were irregular, broken, fumbling, as if designed by the trembling or careless hand of a child .... It was as if a melancholy-mad tenant who ought to have been kept in the topmost chamber of his house had burst through the roof and lifted himself up to the gaze of the world.
>
> (*ibid.*, pp.15-16)

There is no traffic on the road to the Castle: the suspicion begins to form that this is a route designed for one person only, like the door to the Law outside which the man from the country waits and dies in *The Trial*.

> He resumed his walk, but the way proved long. For the street he was in, the main street of the village, did not lead up to the Castle hill, it only made towards it and then, as if deliberately, turned aside, and though it did not lead away from the Castle it got no nearer to it either .... He was also amazed at the length of the village, which seemed to have no end; again and again the same little houses, and frost-bound window panes and snow and the entire absence of human beings.
>
> (*ibid.*, p.17)

In creating this sense that the road to the Castle is uniquely for K., almost the projection of his imagination, Kafka is following to some extent the traditions of earlier quest literature. In some versions of the Grail-quest each knight has a different vision of the Holy Grail, suited to his particular degree of virtue; the road which Christian takes is the King's High Road, but his progress along it is unique since he alone can bring his soul to salvation. But even in this respect Kafka parodies or inverts the traditions: not only does the goal remain inaccessible for K., but he becomes progressively less interested in reaching it, or in proving to the authorities in the Castle that he is the Land-Surveyor. He also becomes less certain that these are his goals, or even possible goals.

A similar dislocation of quest occurs in Hermann Hesse's *Der Steppenwolf*, in which parts of the action – often fantastic or dreamlike – have affinities with allegory. The hero, engaged in some sort of pursuit of identity, enters

> THE MAGIC THEATRE   FOR MADMEN ONLY
> PRICE OF ADMITTANCE YOUR MIND
> NOT FOR EVERYBODY

Previous changes in his character have created the expectation that his experiences in the 'Theatre' will be in some way definitive. The ensuing dislocated experiences and hallucinatory transformations in fact frustrate equally the expectations of readers and hero. He is repeatedly confronted by mirrors offering distorted, fragmented, or dissolving images of himself. Each emblematically labelled door in the Theatre through which he passes precipitates him into some extreme but necessarily partial experience, corresponding to a single element in the composition of his personality. He ends by impulsively killing the girl with whom he entered the Theatre, and to whom he confidently anticipated making love. Though it is implied that the girl and her murder are fantasies, the fact that death is an ingredient in the conclusion of this progress suggests affinities with the endings of *The Trial* and *Frankenstein*, in both of which annihilation is the only possible resolution.

The sharpest distinction between this kind of movement or progress and that which forms the action of *La Divina Commedia*, *The Faerie Queene*, or *The Pilgrim's Progress*, is that in those works some scale of values is accessible by which to judge both the particular and the general significance of any incident. Even *Gulliver's Travels*, a work curiously poised between the confident translucence of 'classic' allegories and the opacity of modern ones, allows the reader some guidance. Gulliver attains what appears to be a state of enlightenment, but this is presented with sufficient irony to ensure that we can see the extent to which it is a parody of genuine enlightenment. In *The Castle* and *Der Steppenwolf*, as in many modern allegories, hierarchy and objectives are both blurred and a source of threat. But it must be emphasized that the distinction between the two kinds of progress is ideological rather than formal. The basic structure of the action is similar in both kinds of allegory, relying on metaphors of progress such as the journey or quest, and on repeated encounters taking the form of dialogue, or combat, or imprisonment.

These forms of action recur because allegory derives in literary-historical terms from the representation of abstractions, and, even when such abstractions are not directly personified, it is based on generalization. An abstraction, whether good or bad, cannot of its nature change. 'Love' may have the power to transform itself, to be represented in several manifestations in the course of the allegory, but it must in essence be immutable if both the word and the concept are not to become meaningless. This essential changelessness can be preserved without loss of variety if the hero and his allies and opponents are shown in a patterned sequence of confrontations. Repetition gives the reader a cumulative under-standing of the abstractions which control the meaning of the allegory, and is also an excellent dramatic means for demonstrating the validity of any ideal. In the second book of *The Faerie Queene* the way in which Guyon reacts to his encounters with Mammon, with Pyrochles, and with Acrasia, shows the ideal of Temperance as a viable guide in responding to the several passions of cupidity, rage, and lust.

In the case of Guyon, his temptations are allegorizations of aspects of his own character or desires, even as the Dreamer's various mentors in *Piers Plowman* are aspects of himself, or the experiences of Harry Haller in the Magic Theatre offer images of the components of his own psyche and its development. In *The Pilgrim's Progress*, Faithful and Hopeful (and indeed Despair) are also generated by the central figure of Christian; they are the qualities or faculties he most needs at a given point in the action (though when Faithful is put to death it does not mean that Christian has lost his faith – the allegorization has there shifted to what happens to the faithful in the world of the flesh). Guyon, as the Knight of Temperance, cannot be shown as merely and continuously temperate, since temperance is a state defined by actions showing equipoise between two polarities. Tension has to be created by showing him as at least in some degree tempted by sensuality or money or the desire for revenge, otherwise his temperance would not be a matter of choice, but of natural immutable character – he would be too much the abstraction Temperance itself, rather than the human though fictional embodiment of the practice of virtue. It is only by retaining some element in the action that corresponds to human experience, and not solely to the abstract patterns of allegorical meaning, that the adventures of the hero can be enlightening to the morally interested reader – or, of course, to the imaginatively interested reader.

The possibilities for continuing this process of moral testing are unlimited. Given the basic fact that abstractions cannot change, their operations and effects could be demonstrated in an endless series of trials, encounters, or battles. In *The Faerie Queene* it is noticeable that the attainment of any one of the heroes' goals is usually the signal for the assignment of further tests. The experiences of Redcrosse in Book I, ix-xii, show this clearly. It is not Contemplation or any of the inmates of the House of Holinesse who counsel final rest, but Despaire:

> What if some litle paine the passage haue,
> That makes fraile flesh to feare the bitter waue?
> Is not short paine well borne, that brings long ease,
> And layes the soule to sleepe in quiet graue?
> Sleepe after toyle, port after stormie seas,
> Ease after warre, death after life does greatly please.

> (I ix 40)

The inertia of the verse, its almost drugged quality, the fact that death brings sleep rather than new life to the soul, all reveal this as false counsel: it is sophistry aimed at making Redcrosse commit suicide. In comparison with the advice offered by his true counsellors it is as perverted as the sensual pleasures of the Bower of Bliss in comparison with the real pleasures of the Garden of Adonis. The 'godly aged Sire' who shows Redcrosse the vision of the New Jerusalem will not allow him to remain in peace for ever, as he desires. Instead he urges on Redcrosse to the completion of the task in hand. And even when the Dragon has been slain, and Una's parents restored to their kingdom, and Redcrosse and Una married, the knight must still return to the court of the Faerie Queene who first laid upon him the charge of destroying the Dragon. The practice of virtue and thus the actions of allegorized virtues are a kind of perpetual motion machine; cessation means impotence.

Many of Spenser's characters are based on the conception of the true knight, an ideal derived from earlier chivalric literature. Of course, Spenser redefines it both in the course of the poem and by claiming for it a contemporary practical application in the letter to Raleigh 'expounding his whole intention': 'The generall end therefore of all the booke is to fashion a gentleman or noble person in vertuous and gentle discipline' (Works, p.407). In Romance, as in ballads and folk tales, the episodic structure is illimitable. Even if a particular passage in a hero's life is given the arbitrary finality of an ending, the story may always be taken up again at another point by another author. In this sort of literature, especially in such popular Romances as King Horn and Havelok where love is of secondary importance, the hero is most truly himself when in pursuit of something, or engaged in defeating or outwitting an opponent. The later courtly Romances, in which love is a principal element in the story, also show an extreme simplification of character. Spenser's knights, and indeed most allegorical heroes, are like the heroes of Romance in being most themselves when in pursuit of an object or struggling with their enemies. In this, Romance and allegory differ sharply from sentimental novels or comedies in which the home-coming, getting the girl, winning the inheritance, is not only the culmination of the action, but also the point at which the hero or heroine are most fully realized. Their identities triumph in the ending. In the last chapter of Little Dorrit, her marriage is recorded in the same Parish Registers as her birth:

> 'this young lady ... has come now to the third volume of our
> Registers. Her birth is in what I call the first volume; she lay
> asleep on this very floor, with her pretty head on what I
> call the second volume; and she's now a-writing her little name
> as a bride, in what I call the third volume.'

Little Dorrit and Arthur Clennam are 'inseparable and blessed'. They have attained what they need in the fixed and limited. It is interesting that Hard Times, the novel in which Dickens is most nearly allegorical, has a very inconclusive conclusion in comparison with Little Dorrit. The final chapters include the death of the only character who might be seen as the hero, failed adultery, permanent separation without divorce, the wrong-doer discovered but unpunished, and the circus (from which the action began in opposition to the destructive stasis of Gradgrind's school) continuing on its way.

Some allegories seem to have a definite ending – for example, *The Pilgrim's Progress*. But the ending here is absolute because it is an ideal home-coming, out of time. Christian loses his identity to become one of the Blessed. Yet even Bunyan felt the need to continue the same allegorical narrative by telling of the progress of Christiana and the children. In *Piers Plowman* the vision of the Harrowing of Hell, in which a divine order is most successfully imposed on history's imperfections, is not conclusive but climactic. It is immediately followed by the attacks of Antichrist on the Church. The poem ends in both the B text and the third and final C text with Conscience announcing his intention to become a pilgrim and search for Piers the Ploughman. Since Piers has already been 'found' this obviously signals the perpetuity of the allegorical act of pilgrimage. In the *Paradiso* Dante's last vision is not finite or final:

> All'alta fantasia qui mancò possa;
>   ma già volgeva il mio disio e 'l velle
>   sì come rota ch'igualmente è mossa'
>
> l'amor che move il sole e l'altre stelle.
>
> (Here I lack power for this high fantasy, but already my
> desire and will turned like a wheel, moved equally by the
> love that moves the sun and the other stars.)

The verbs of movement, *volgeva*, *è mossa*, *move*, emphasize the continuity of divine action, and the action of the poem and the impulse which generated it. Allegories can only show the sense of an ending by invoking a hierarchy of values, in which a supreme power can function as a *deus ex machina* and give some sort of termination to the action. When this hierarchy is absent, so also is an ending – as in *The Trial* and *The Castle*. And even *The Faerie Queene* and de Lorris's *Le Roman de la Rose* are both unfinished, though they include such hierarchies of power and value.

The repetition of similar incidents and the episodic structure of allegory derive from the need to present abstract principles as fundamentally unchanging but applicable in diverse contexts. The recurrence of certain overall structures such as the quest can perhaps be explained by the need to expound the system within which the abstractions function. Allegory requires not only an episodic narrative which can be extended at will, but also means for the analysis of that narrative. Exposition must co-exist with the dramatized substance of the exposition. A form which ideally meets this requirement is the journey, a metaphor for life which can be found at almost all periods of western culture. In the Middle Ages it was given additional popularity by the common practice of pilgrimage: De Guileville's *Pèlerinage de la Vie Humaine*, though one of the most extensive, is only one of many allegories that exploit the metaphor of an eventful journey given purpose by a holy objective.

The chivalric quest is the basis of much medieval literature both popular and courtly, and this provided allegory with a useful narrative model. When the form declined the model became increasingly unusable: Spenser, writing with the extraordinary nostalgic 'chivalry' of the Tudor court in the background, was perhaps the last allegorist who could have used it with ease, and then only at the price of some rather strained archaizing. But the *idea* of the quest survived, and the pilgrimage and the fantastic journey are analogies to it which are perhaps more durable because less rooted in a particular kind of society. In journey, as in dream-vision, the traveller is an instrument whereby systems can be explored. Because he is an outsider he often possesses a special kind of objectivity about the newly encountered system as a whole, while the sequential nature of his experiences provides for explaining its particularities. Everything encountered is new and strange, and so the questions asked by the traveller are a natural pretext for explanation whether he is a naïf or not. Such explanation, especially if occasioned by ideological considerations rather than by the material demands of the plot, sits very uncomfortably in the middle of naturalistic fiction. The problem can be observed in Robert Tressell's novel, *The Ragged-Trousered Philanthropists*, which it is difficult to judge simultaneously by ideological and literary criteria. The lucid expositions of socialism threaten to swamp the narrative, while the account of the lives of the house-painters working in a small seaside town before the First World War has a vitality which distracts from the necessarily drier expository passages. In the case of the journey or voyage the ideological and the naturalistic can be more satisfactorily compounded. The act of travelling, like the succession of *aventures* in Romance, is theoretically illimitable, and so consequently are the opportunities for didactic analysis. The Utopia and the Dystopia both entail a degree of allegorization, the first of ideal principles, the second of hostile ones; both have always made use of the figure of an outsider, generally a traveller.

In More's *Utopia* the account of the island is given by Raphael Hythloday, who sailed 'not as the mariner Palinurus, but as the expert and prudent prince Ulysses; yea, rather as the ancient and sage philosopher Plato'. (The reference to Ulysses suggests one of the obvious ancestors for the literature of the journey.) More prefixes the account of Utopia itself with an imaginary dialogue between himself and Hythloday about matters of law and custom which would have been of interest to every contemporary Englishman: capital punishment for theft, the parasitism of the rich, rackrenting, standing armies, enclosures, royal revenues, the limitation of royal capital. This dialogue establishes the intelligence of Hythloday, thus giving greater authority to his narrative, and it also encourages the reader to make comparisons between the ideal commonwealth and the way in which European government actually functions.

Gulliver's Travels and *Brave New World* both rely on the convention of the alien traveller in a utopian/dystopian society, but the movement between the fictional and the actual is less explicitly pointed than it is in *Utopia*. In both books adverse criticisms of societies are offered obliquely via the allegorical action, but neither Swift nor Huxley presents the practical basis for a state in fictional form, as Thomas More does. Though Gulliver's discussions with his Houyhnhnm master do entail comparisons between early eighteenth-century Europe and the idealized community of horses, two factors make the more urgent problems of social organization somewhat remote. First, the moral perfection of the Houyhnhnms disallows the possibility of crime. The presence of evil in human nature is represented by the Yahoos: as a result the problem is formulated in terms of the efficient control of an inferior race, rather than of the accommodation of faulty human nature in a just society. Second, the semi-pastoral and archaic nature of the Houyhnhnms' society absolves Swift from the consideration of economic matters: in *Utopia*, More at least attempts to offer the rudiments of an ideal economy.

In Mary Shelley's *Frankenstein* the monster (like Gulliver and the

Savage) also confronts and comments on totally unfamiliar situations in the course of his wanderings. Of course, his alien nature and status as an outsider are emphasized for the sake of tragic, as much as didactic, effect. The reported action of the allegory exists in order to give us insight into the nature of the monster's sufferings: the monster does not exist primarily as a vehicle for comment upon the world. To achieve this balance between tragedy and social comment, one of the usual procedures of allegory is reversed to brilliant effect – instead of exposing a credible and realistic hero to a journey through an extraordinary allegorical world, she shows us an incredible and unreal traveller confronting the everyday world and commenting upon that. His bitter observations on the nature of human affections and responses do not express a satirical didacticism on the part of the author. He is bitter because his monstrous appearance separates him irrevocably from human contact; it is this separateness that makes him both the ideal vehicle for comment and the perfect expression of the moral issues with which the allegory is concerned. The device of the alien traveller is modified to deal with dilemmas that have individual or mythic focus, rather than a social one.

As in many allegories, the use of this device entails another common feature of allegorical action: commentary upon the narrative, which comes not only from the creature as he tells his story to Victor Frankenstein, but also from Frankenstein himself as he narrates his autobiography to the explorer, Robert Walton. The central events of the allegory are thus enclosed within three layers of interpretation – from the monster, from Frankenstein, and from Walton. All three of them are in some degree unusually distanced from the world, whether by fate, accident, or desire. Each is an inveterate journeyer from necessity, terror, or ambition. Mary Shelley thus modifies the device of the alien traveller to achieve effects different from those of *Gulliver's Travels* or *Brave New World*: but in all these works the responses of an individual whose origins are external to the society he describes offer the stimuli for analysis. What is even more important, in the context of this argument, is that our awareness of the allegorical element in these works derives very much from the thread of commentary coming from an outsider observing the action. Christian, Calidore, and Dante are similarly offered commentary to help them confront the experiences for which nothing previously has prepared them, and this commentary upon the events occurring in some kind of journey is crucial to the integration of the allegorical fiction with its significance.

The journey is a very rich and pliable metaphor, a means of expressing complex kinds of movement; in literary forms which are based on more limited metaphors, such as the masque, the procession or progress, and the debate poem, we can see allegorical movement at its most simple. These forms may be autonomous: Dunbar's *The Goldyn Targe* and *The Dance of the Sevin Deidly Synnis*, or any of the anonymous poems on the Ship of State, are examples of small-scale anatomies. Such emblematic ways of conveying allegorical meaning also occur as part of larger allegories, as in the confession of the seven deadly sins in *Piers Plowman*, or the sinister masque of Cupid in the House of Busyrane (*Faerie Queene*, III ix). Generally, where these forms are self-contained, the observer is uninvolved, serving only as a notional audience, or (in medieval literature) as that kind of passive dreamer who is offered a demonstration of a particular set of relationships without initiating or participating in the movement.

In the debate poem it is possible to see a highly simplistic form of allegory in which the antagonisms and oppositions of allegorical warfare combine with the movement of the masque or progress. The various arguments and counter-arguments of Soul and Body, Wine and Water, or Owl and Nightingale (roughly, sacred versus profane love), function in the same way as the various stages in a combat or the separate episodes in a quest or journey. They do not provide in themselves any solution, since the opposing parties are eternally separate for linguistic reasons, if no other. Ultimately, stichomythia becomes very boring; the thread of argument in debate, as the act of procession or dance, provides only the illusion of progress. Self-contained masque or debate is only a thinly allegorized form of exposition, but when the rituals of debate and progress are subordinated to the larger narrative patterns of complex allegories, they become valuable contributory elements. The questions and answers in a debate occurring within a fully elaborated allegory are significant not only in respect of the particular argument but also because they can be cross-referenced to the more comprehensive meaning of the whole. Thus in *Piers Plowman* it is not at issue whether Study should take precedence over Wit, but what they may both contribute towards discovering

a model of the good life, or to the individual pursuit of salvation.
When Britomartis sees the masque of Cupid, it is not simply a
demonstration of the destructive power of Love, but also a test of
her fortitude as the personification of Chastity. The masque offers
her the opportunity to break the power which has imprisoned and
tortured Amoret, since the door behind which Busyrane holds
Amoret only opens at the advent of the nightly procession. Britomartis must intervene and be wounded herself before Amoret can
be freed and the power of the enchanter (and, allegorically, of a
cruel Cupid) be 'cleane subuerst'.

An almost doctrinaire rigidity and absence of any real progress
are the limitations of autonomous masque, procession, or debate,
and they are also apparent in allegorical warfare. One of the
clearest examples is to be found in Prudentius' *Psychomachia*
(which Coleridge called the first allegory completely modern in its
form). C. S. Lewis commented that:

> While it is true that the *bellum intestinum* is the root of all
> allegory, it is no less true that only the crudest allegory will
> represent it by a pitched battle. The abstractions owe their
> life to the inner conflict; but when once they have come to
> life, the poet must fetch a compass and dispose his fiction more
> artfully if he is to succeed.
>
> (*Allegory of Love*, p.68)

He added that Seneca with his imagery of life as journey was
nearer the mark than Prudentius, because the journey offered 'the
perennial strangeness, the adventurousness, and the sinuous forward
movement of the inner life'. Having chosen the narrative form of a
battle between the Virtues and Vices for the soul of man, the possible endings for the allegory are severely limited: Virtue wins,
Vice wins, or the battle is inconclusive. The moralistic intentions
of most allegorists usually precludes any outcome but the first.
Prudentius imagined the source of the poem more clearly than the
restrictions of its narrative form:

> fervent bella horrida, fervent
> ossibus inclusa, fremit et discordibus armis
> non simplex natura hominis; nam viscera limo
> effigiata premunt animam.
>
> (*Psychomachia*, 902-5)

(Horrid war rages, rages within the bones, and the double
nature of man sounds with armed discord; for flesh, formed
out of clay, presses upon the soul.)

This discord is the substance of Marvell's 'A Dialogue between the
Soul and Body':

O who shall, from this Dungeon, raise
A Soul inslav'd so many wayes?
With bolts of Bones, that fetter'd stands
In Feet; and manacled in Hands. ...

O who shall me deliver whole,
From bonds of this Tyrannic Soul?
Which, stretcht upright, impales me so,
That mine own Precipice I go;

All allegory attempts to escape the pressures and the tormenting
relativity of the material and contingent by giving form to the
ideal and the abstract. Unfortunately, Prudentius' extended metaphor of legionary combat is simply too inelastic to express the
diversities of *non simplex natura*, and moreover there is insuperable
impropriety in involving the Virtues in armed combat. Prudentius
was only able to make Humilitas and Patientia triumph by
distinctly un-military means, thus contradicting the high valuation
of heroism which the combative metaphor entails.

It has been suggested that the recurrent forms of allegorical
action, quest, journey, masque or procession, debate, battle, all
involve a high degree of patterned repetition. In order to demonstrate effectively how an ideal or a principle should operate the
allegorist shows it in action in several different but basically
comparable situations. Christian has to escape from the castle of
Giant Despair with the help of Hopeful, or from the fiend Apollyon
by reliance on his armour with its spiritual significances. The Love
in *Le Roman de la Rose* must be capable of overcoming the hostility
of Danger or of Jealousy, who builds a castle in which to immure
the Rose and Bialacoil (Sweet Welcome). All the obstacles are
repeated variants of the same theme – the difficulty of winning the
Rose, i.e. the love of the chosen woman. Should the allegorist use
any one of the possible narrative forms in isolation rather than
as part of a multifarious action, the repetitiousness is often over-

whelmingly obvious. The necessary restrictions of the basic metaphors of debate or battle make it impossible for the similarity
between each episode to be concealed, and if some hierarchy is
invoked to provide an ending (as that Virtue is superior to Vice and
must therefore triumph), this can only be done at the cost of
obvious arbitrariness.

There is however one recurrent element in allegorical writing
that prevents the action from becoming a seemingly endless process
with the overall effect of stasis: a belief in the possibility of transformation. This possibility underlies a great deal of literature, it is
true, but in allegory it has an obvious didactic basis. If the author
believes that his readers can be changed and made wiser by the
meaning of his work, then one of the most effective ways for him to
demonstrate this is to show his heroes transformed by their experience of the action, upon which the meaning depends. One of the
obvious advantages of the journey metaphor lies in answering to
this belief, for the journeyer is necessarily transformed by the act of
journeying: even Quixote is changed in some degree, though he
preserves (until his death-bed) his fundamental ideals and thus his
quasi-allegoric function. At the least, the allegorist can change
or modify his readers' perceptions of the relationships between the
allegorized elements by the effect of sequence during a procession
or debate. This is effected by the simple fact of b coming after a,
or of x being paired with y. If Pride leads the procession, or rides
in a chariot drawn by the six other Sins (as in *Faerie Queene*,
I iv), this must suggest that this vice is dominant, whether this
is explicitly stated or not. Even where the protagonists cannot
change without ceasing to be themselves, the perceptions of the
observer and reader are changed by exposure to the sequence of
the allegorical action.

In *The Pilgrim's Progress* Christian is transformed by his difficult
journey (his life-long struggle) into a being worthy to inherit
eternal life. At this point, he loses his allegorical identity and
becomes one of a company. He becomes most what he is, Christian,
by a series of victories, and having become purely Christian, ceases
to exist in terms of allegorized human experience. In the river
of Death Christian and Hopeful shed mortality, for they 'left their
Mortal Garments behind them in the River: for though they went in
with them, they came out without them', and as they pass into the
City 'they were transfigured, and they had Raiment put on that

shone like Gold'. In *Piers Plowman*, Piers is revealed in a series of allegorical roles, each one an intensification of the last. When metamorphosed into Christ he ceases to be solely the object of the Dreamer's quest, and becomes a figure in an historical drama. This transformation offers a correlative to the changes taking place in the Dreamer, who turns during the episodes of waking life linking the various stages of the vision into an increasingly outcast figure. He begins dressed in ragged clothes like a shepherd or 'an heremite', and becomes poorer, shabbier, colder, almost starving, and even appearing insane to hostile observers. These external changes mark not only the increasing urgency of the quest, but suggest the *sancta simplicitas* of the outcast fool who possesses inwardly some kind of divine knowledge. As the Dreamer grows more sharply aware of what he should be looking for, so the figure that is the object of the quest is transformed.

In James Hogg's *The Private Memoirs and Confessions of a Justified Sinner*, the 'justified sinner' Robert Wringhim is also changed and sees changed things. In the first half of the book, which is presented as straight reported narrative, he appears the type of perverted religious fanatic who uses theological sophistries to justify criminal acts. When he becomes his own chronicler he appears not only progressively more human, but also changes his allegorical function to become any man destroyed by his own delusions. While Wringhim becomes human, more of an Everyman figure, his 'sanguine friend' is revealed as the Devil. As in *Piers Plowman*, the ability to evaluate correctly is echoed by transformations in the objects perceived. Starting as the pursuer, he becomes the pursued; his chief assistant in the destruction of his brother becomes the instrument of his own pursuit and destruction. A comparable point is made by the way in which Frankenstein's monster changes his role from that of brain-child to destroyer.

The idea of transformation is most literally expressed in metamorphosis. In myths, physical transformation indicates a change in function: for the archaeologist or anthropologist this often has cultural significance, such as for example the subordination of one race or culture with its own particular rites and deities by another, which then assimilates the customs of the conquered. In Greek myth, the fate of Hermaphroditus (or Androgyne) suggests both those individuals who are double-sexed and the transitional period between matriarchy and patriarchy; Athene's transformation of

Arachne into a spider because she was jealous of the skill in weaving which had brought her fame throughout Lydia, is probably connected with the commercial rivalry over the control of the textile trade in the Aegean. It is noticeable that persons or objects transformed always preserve some of their original characteristics, either of appearance or of behaviour: Hermaphroditus and Androgyne retain the genitals of one sex while assuming the secondary characteristics of the other such as breasts or a beard. Arachne as a spider continues to spin and weave as she did when human; Philomela, metamorphosed into a nightingale, continues to complain of her rape by Tereus. Metempsychosis, the same soul in a different body, is often of more interest to the allegorist than complete physical transformation. This enables the basic allegorical function of a character to be preserved, while giving them additional narrative or dramatic roles. The idea that was first represented in one form becomes inevitably associated with the superadded ideas represented in the later form. This is very clear in the Piers/Christ transformation – God in human form becomes linked with the ideal of plebeian and rural simplicity.

The immense influence of Ovid's *Metamorphoses* on medieval and renaissance literature, its status as one of the principal sources of classical mythology, is well known. Allegory is much indebted to the Ovidian tradition for both particular examples of transformation and for wider conceptions of their significance. Dante places Ovid in the highest place in the underworld possible for a pagan poet, and there are constant references to the *Metamorphoses* in *La Divina Commedia*. Chaucer not only borrowed material from Ovid, but was obviously in sympathy with the tone and style of his work: *The House of Fame*, *The Legend of Good Women*, and tales such as the *Manciple's Tale* all reveal his influence.

The Faerie Queene offers a complex example of the allegorist's interest in transformation, since apart from the progressive moral modification of the heroes by means of testing, there are also numerous actual metamorphoses. Some of these are Ovidian allusions, but Spenser goes further and invents some of his own. Whereas the partial spiritual transformations, resulting from the continued exercise of virtue, are beneficial, total physical meta- effects. Archimago can make himself appear a hermit or a pilgrim morphosis always derives from evil intentions and is evil in its in order to mislead his virtuous opponents. Duessa conceals her 'partes misshapen, monstruous' and appears as a beautiful woman, deceiving Fradubio, Redcrosse, and Sansfoy and his brothers; even Night herself does not recognize the transformed Duessa:

> In that faire face
> The false resemblance of Deceipt, I wist
> Did closely lurke; yet so true-seeming grace
> It carried, that I scarse in darkesome place
> Could it discerne, though I the mother bee
> Of falshood and root of *Duessaes* race.

(I v 27)

The false Florimell, made out of snow by the witch, deludes even those who have loved the real Florimell. Suitably enough, at the end of the tournament in Book IV, Cantos iv and v, she chooses the false knight Braggadocchio, whose appearance is the only thing about him that could remotely be called knightly. Since the possibility of distinguishing good from evil is a central concern of the poem, such transformations are additional means by which the virtuous are tested; all the Spenserian metamorphoses relate to the preoccupation with the difference between appearance and reality. This preoccupation is also expressed in characters such as the Salvage Man, who appears rough and violent but is truly gentle, or Britomartis who seems a male knight but is a woman, or in the experiences of Calidore who learns true courtesy in becoming a member of a pastoral community. He learns that courtesy is not solely the prerogative of courts, as might appear, but can and perhaps should be learnt in an altogether rustic environment.

In Kafka, predictably, the effects of metamorphosis are considered in terms of the internal, psychological effects of transformation. In *Metamorphosis*, the physical change of Gregor Samsa into a beetle has already occurred at the beginning of the story. The process is thus retrospective, the action of the story being the change in Gregor's mind from that of a man who happens to have acquired the body of a beetle, to that of a being more entirely beetle-ish. The responses of his family to the transformation convey the suggestion that love is entirely dependent upon the maintenance of convention, that families will happily be parasitic upon one member and yet refuse to support that member should he need it, and that sibling rivalry is more than a psychologist's fiction – Gregor's sister becomes prettier, more nubile, from the moment the family go off on a journey to celebrate the disposal of the beetle-carcass by the charwoman.

The duality of response with which a metamorphosed character such as the Samsa-beetle must be approached is comparable to the ambiguity of Archimago-Hermit or Duessa-Fidessa for the other characters in *The Faerie Queene*. Gregor feels like a beetle, longing to hide under the sofa or to mumble rancid scraps of food, but he is able to introspect and verbalize like a man: he is emotively beetle but conceptually man. This doubleness forces an allegorical reading of his situation and that progression from the particular to the general which is characteristic of allegorical interpretation. The imprisonment of a human consciousness within the body of an insect is a metaphor for much of our experience as human beings (The 'soul inslav'd' again). If he becomes more beetle-ish because he looks like a beetle and is consequently treated like one, would not the same change of consciousness afflict anyone who suffered a violent transformation of environment? (The Marxist dictum that 'environment determines consciousness' comes to mind – in this case the externals of the body are to be seen as part of environment.) Metamorphosis has here no moral causality, as one might expect from Kafka, with his systematic denial of hierarchies of value in the external world. By contrast, when Fradubio is imprisoned in a tree (*Faerie Queene*, I ii) it is the result of his having preferred Duessa to his own 'gentle Lady', Fraelissa. He puts himself into the power of an evil agent by exercising judgment wrongly, and is therefore deprived of the right to judge or act by being transformed into a tree (a negative version of the myth of Baucis and Philemon). Calidore's transformation from knight to shepherd in Book VI of *The Faerie Queene* is different from Fradubio's in being voluntary, but it too has a moral origin and consequence; limiting himself to a sphere of action apparently more restricted than his normal one, Calidore is offered perceptions and insights (not least importantly the vision of the Graces dancing to Colin Clout's music), which make him more than he was. Change of function is here expansive.

The two directions in which transformations may work in allegories, either towards greater freedom or towards imprisonment and fixity (the beetle trapped in a single room is only a short step from the beetle pinned in a specimen case) reflect the paradox suggested in the common forms of allegorical action. The narrative form of many allegories appears to display incompatible tendencies: towards the repetition of structurally similar incidents, which produces the effect of immobility, and towards some kind of large-scale movement, which suggests the possibility of radical change. These paradoxical tendencies derive from the fact that most allegories are trying to achieve two kinds of effect. On the one hand, the allegorist wishes to create or reflect an imagined model of the universe, or of the psyche, or of the forces operating in human society. This model must be clear or it will be ineffectual as a didactic or ideological demonstration; and it must be capable of generalization, or the abstract significance of the allegory will be submerged by the particularities of the action. To achieve clarity, the action needs to be schematized, almost diagrammatic, and this results in a considerable degree of repetition and the obvious polarization of opposing forces. When an allegory relies primarily on a single form of action, be it battle or debate, it has this clarity – often at the expense of subtlety. It will also tend to be dualistic, if not almost Manichean, in that Good has to be presented in terms comparable with Evil if it is to engage with it at all (this is the problem that confronted Prudentius; Spenser's 'fair-seeming' villains, deceiving even the heroes, are a more subtle way of coming to terms with it).

However, the allegorist wants to convey to his readers something more than the impression of a closed system in which the intrinsic qualities or principles that are allegorized are unchanging in themselves and in relation to one another – a kind of *perpetuum mobile* which suggests unshakeable equilibrium. Here the other half of the ambitions of the writer of allegory comes into play: his concern with process, with progression. For the literary or secular allegorist the anagogic significance of the action is as important as it was for the medieval theologian interpreting sacred biblical action. Hence the recurrence of forms such as the journey or the quest, with their emphasis on directed energy, and on the progressive evolution, education, and enlightenment of the heroes. A mixed form offers a means of satisfying both aspects of the allegorist's intentions: the action is based on a large-scale fluid metaphor, such as the journey or the process of law, but incorporates other more schematic devices like the masque or debate or battle. It also has immense possibilities for the inclusion of a Rabelaisian diversity of objects and occurrences.

Allegories at their best can combine diversity of images or allusions with the intellectual satisfactions of a rationally structured and ordered action (as in a Shakespeare play). Concerned with linear movement, they also are made clearer and more diverse by including digressions. Sterne's observations, *à propos* of drawing Uncle Toby's character while simultaneously telling us about Aunt Dinah and the coachman, are highly pertinent:

> By this contrivance the machinery of my work is of a species by itself; two contrary motions are introduced into it, and reconciled, which were thought to be at variance with each other. In a word, my work is digressive, and it is progressive too, – and at the same time.
>
> ... from the beginning of this, you see, I have constructed the main work and the adventitious parts of it with such intersections, and have so complicated and involved the digressive and progressive movements, one wheel within another, that the whole machine, in general, has been kept a-going....
>
> (*Tristram Shandy*, I XXII, p.101)

2
A pleasing analysis: techniques of persuasion and elucidation

1   *The reader as participant*

In the previous chapter I have suggested that the recurrent narrative metaphors and episodic structure of allegory derive from a particular non-mimetic choice of subject matter, and from the attempt to express the particular and the general simultaneously. However, to write allegorically is not merely to create a particular kind of literature, but also to make assumptions about its function and about a particular way of reading. In considering the mode we need to attend to the audience as well as to individual works. Many writers of allegory have commented in prefaces or in the body of their works on the response they expect from their readers, and these expectations control both the detailed local texture of allegory and the values and images which form a central and schematized core of meaning.

Allegory, like myth, presupposes an audience who will respond to it in specific ways: to consider its authors' conception of this response is not necessarily to indulge in the 'intentional fallacy'. Critics like W. K. Wimsatt have quite properly attacked the critical method which extrapolates the author's intentions from biographical and other evidence and bases both interpretation and evaluation upon them. It is a different matter to pay attention to allegorists' views of how their readers may and should react, since this is to acknowledge one of the characteristic features of the mode, rather than to use the individual identity of an author as a criterion for judging his work.

A didactic and expository mode cannot flourish without an

audience that regards literature as a viable and natural vehicle for teaching, since it presupposes readers prepared to learn from a poem or story. Many circumstances, the allegorical interpretation of the Bible among them, allowed medieval authors to assume that one of the proper functions of their work was to assist moral speculation and decision. From this arises one of the great virtues of medieval literature, its open and unembarrassed attention to the moral value of the subject matter, even though the other side of this coin is that many lesser works now seem laboured and hectoring in their insistence on didactic purpose. A great medieval writer like Chaucer or Dante could assume a constant interplay between his work and the responses of those reading it: without embarrassment he could turn aside from the course of the story and discuss the way in which they are responding to that story as it unfolds. This creates a curious sense of intimacy between creator and recipient: you may think, says Chaucer, that Troilus's behaviour when he falls in love with Criseyde is strange; but you know that ways of acting and speaking change in the course of years even though men have similar desires; the conventions of love change yet men still experience the emotion. This dialogue with the audience differs from authorial digressions in, for example, nineteenth-century novels in that it leads away from the work, and is not aimed at asserting either the reality of the characters or the truthfulness of the author's record of them. It specifically deflects us from thinking only about the particular way in which one individual fell in love and suffered for it, and makes us attend to a more general view of loving: why we do it, how it affects us and our view of the world, how it relates to other experiences and values. The acknowledgment of the artifice of the work, its status as only one way of looking at the world, liberates us from the particular into the general. Such a movement is of course also characteristic of allegory, and it is therefore not surprising that allegory was vigorous in a climate where all literature encouraged readers to look beyond the specific.

Medieval authors could be didactic without being disagreeable because the idea of literature as advisory was familiar and accepted. Readers and listeners were accustomed to partially or entirely allegorical forms like the dream vision, and to the notion that they contained meanings and values that could have practical application to their own lives. They were also familiar with the allegorical interpretation of the Bible and of sacred and patristic texts. This medieval discipline of exegesis has often been confused with allegory itself, and the confusion has contributed to a conception of allegory as an aridly scholastic mode. The two should be distinguished since the manner in which medieval scholars interpreted the Bible is first and foremost a critical method with theological objectives. It has nothing to do with ways of writing the kind of allegorical literature which concerns this book. Starting with a given, a sacred text, the critic attempted to draw forth from it the maximum possible theological and moral significance, using both his own interpretative abilities and his knowledge of traditional interpretations. Especially in the case of certain Old Testament events these traditions were invariable: the burning bush from which God spoke to Moses, the rod of Jesse, and Gideon's fleece miraculously covered with dew were all types of the Virgin Mary and of the Immaculate Conception. It is important to remember that the texts interpreted in this way were sacred texts, regardless of whether the exegete used traditional meanings or more novel and idiosyncratic ones. No medieval allegorist would have believed that it was possible for him to compose a work with the same intensity or complexity of meaning as a biblical or even a patristic text. The frequently quoted *Letter to Can Grande* (whether or not it can be confidently attributed to Dante) further confused the issue by seeming to claim for secular literary works the same four levels of meaning believed to exist in Scripture: the literal, allegorical, tropological, and anagogical. But Dante or the author is careful to distinguish between poets and theologians, and between the ways in which poets indicate meaning and those by which theologians discover them in divinely inspired books. Any attempt to read in this way even religious allegories of the period (like *La Divina Commedia* itself or *Piers Plowman*) rapidly breaks down.

While allegorical exegesis as a part of theology needs to be distinguished from allegory as literature, it obviously encouraged the understanding and enjoyment of the latter at the medieval period. As a method of reading sacred texts it was vigorous and ubiquitous. It strengthened certain habits of mind, among them the expectation that the most featureless surface could be made to yield up profound significance, the readiness to apprehend double meanings simultaneously, and perhaps above all the belief that pleasure and

instruction were not separable. Time and again in medieval literature references occur to the grain that can be extracted from the
chaff of words, to the fact that everything that is written may teach
us something, to the delight in discovering *sentence* or meaning.
The Host in *The Canterbury Tales* could hardly be seen as the type
of scholastic critic, yet he demands a tale in which there is 'som
murthe *or som doctryne*' when he silences the pilgrim Chaucer's
Sir Thopas. The 'moral tale vertuous' which answers his demand is
the prose allegory of Melibee and his wife Dame Prudence. It relies
almost entirely on moral debate and the citation of authorities
in support of various arguments. But the Host does not complain
as he did of the vacuities of *Sir Thopas*, which as a Romance
(however bastard) represents a common medieval form of 'enter-
taining' literature. Instead he immediately applies the counsels of
Dame Prudence against violence and vengefulness to his own
domestic situation.

This is admittedly a fictional incident and at least partially ironic.
It could not by itself be used as evidence of a common response to
allegory. But it is not unique, and factual and historical evidence
can be found to supplement such literary allusions. A large proportion of medieval works were allegorical; these exist in a surprising number of copies; they enjoyed wide geographical and
social distribution; and they continued to be copied and circulated
for a considerable period of time. Thus both *Piers Plowman* (in
England) and *Le Roman de la Rose* (throughout Europe) reappear
with a frequency which suggests a widespread enthusiasm for
works conveying at least a certain amount of instruction via an
allegorical action. Such evidence indicates that allegory was
enjoyed and understood by a large audience, and it is therefore not
surprising that apologies for using it are rare, even though humble
apologetics were then almost a reflex of authorial rhetoric. When
the discipline of scriptural exegesis declined in later centuries, the
Christian author addressing allegory to a Christian audience continued to find both a model and a justification for the use of 'types,
shadows, and metaphors' in the Bible; the imagery of the sermons of
Donne and Lancelot Andrewes has its ancestry in the allegorical
interpretation of the Scriptures.

The aptitude of readers for continuous and carefully selective
interpretation is important in understanding the methods of earlier
allegories. When the Lover in *Le Roman de la Rose* looks into

the fountain in the Garden of Mirth he sees two crystal stones (eyes) and the reflection of the Rose, the woman he determines to love. Immediately de Lorris adds:

> This is the mirrour perilous,
> In which the proude Narcisus
> Saw all his face fair and bright ...
> For whoso loketh in that mirrour,
> Ther may nothyng ben his socour. ...
>
> (translation attributed to Chaucer, ll. 1601-6)

This suggests that loving entails self-knowledge as well as knowledge of the person loved, and that it is a dangerous experience. It does not mean that the mere sight of the beloved will cause the Lover to fall into a hopeless state of self-obsession from which death is the only escape. The context of the reference to Narcissus makes it clear that only part of the meaning of Ovid's story is relevant. The reader has to select the notion of danger and the idea that love almost always entails some element of self-projection, and discard the other possible significances of the myth. Actually the degree of control exercised by the allegory over the image of the fountain makes this selection comparatively easy.

A similar sort of selectivity is needed in interpreting incidents in *The Faerie Queene*. The hero of Book v is Artegall, a figure of Justice. His 'glorie is to aide all suppliants pore', and he is on a quest to aid a 'distressed Dame'. Yet he still orders the destruction of Lady Munera and the execution is carried out by his iron servant, Talus:

> Who rudely hayld her forth without remorse,
> Still holding vp her suppliant hands on hye,
> And kneeling at his feet submissiuely.
> But he her suppliant hands, those hands of gold,
> And eke her feete, those feete of siluer trye,
> Which sought vnrighteousnesse, and iustice sold,
> Chopt off, and nayld on high, that all might them behold.
>
> Her selfe then tooke he by the sclender wast,
> In vaine loude crying, and into the flood
> Ouer the Castle wall adowne her cast,
> And there her drowned in the durty mud. ...
>
> (v ii 26-7)

The savage insistence of the language makes this at first sight appear entirely inappropriate behaviour on the part of one who ought to aid women as part of his knightly code, and listen to the pleas of suppliants as his particular virtue. But the equation of Artegall with justice makes it impossible to think of it simply as a cruel act, and leads us to interpret this as representing the way in which a just ruler or nation ought assiduously to destroy anything which makes it possible for bribes and monetary rewards to pervert the course of justice. Had Spenser not relied on the interpretative abilities of his readers the problem of the relationship between money and justice would have been unexpressed, or expressed less succinctly. Without that reliance, the 'good' characters in a didactic work would have to be shown as consistently performing acts which are in absolute terms good. Orwell said when writing about *Gulliver's Travels* in 'Politics vs. Literature' that 'to be occasionally inconsistent is almost a mark of vitality in Utopia books' (*Inside the Whale*, p.129), and the same is true of allegories. Too great a degree of consistency can produce works in which the overall meaning tyrannizes the separate parts into a flat conformism. But inconsistency is hazardous without readers willing and able to interpret selectively.

De Lorris says that his work is called 'the Romance of the Rose,/ In which al the art of love I close'. An art, a particular kind of knowledge is enclosed in the work even as the experience of that art is enclosed in the garden which forms the setting of the action. Neither he nor Langland is in the least defensive about using allegory, whereas both Spenser and Bunyan attempt some kind of justification for doing so. Already, it would seem, it has become difficult for authors to count on their readers as an earlier allegorist might. The justifications turn as much on assumptions about the desires and capabilities of their readers as they do on the formal value of allegory. Bunyan asks:

> Dost thou love picking-meat? Or would'st thou see
> A man i'the Clouds, and hear him speak to thee?

This same quotation (from the 'Author's Apology' prefaced to *The Pilgrim's Progress*) is used by Mervyn Peake as an epigraph to his *Gormenghast* trilogy, a work with strong allegorical affinities. It contains in essence the intentions of every allegorist. He assumes that his readers will be prepared to pick the body of his work for meat, or that if they are not they won't be reading it or continue to read it. Spenser's letter to Raleigh deflects potential critics by suggesting that they can easily find other literature more pleasing.

> To some I know this Methode will seem displesaunt, which had rather haue good discipline deliuered plainly in way of precepts, or sermoned at large ... then thus clowdily enwrapped in Allegoricall deuises. But such, me seeme, should be satisfide with the use of these dayes, seeing all things accounted by their showes, and nothing esteemed of, that is not delightfull and pleasing to commune sence.
>
> (*Works*, p.407)

'Commune sence' has here the sixteenth-century meaning of 'ordinary, average perceptiveness', rather than the implicit approbation of its modern use: Spenser is thus implying that the antagonists of allegory have a taste for the blunt or facile. He also suggests that it is possible for his contemporaries to regard allegory as old-fashioned, and by implication that those who enjoy it will have a respect for the traditional and antique. In the same place Spenser describes *The Faerie Queene* as 'a continued Allegory, or darke conceit' – one of the rare occasions when he uses 'dark' with favourable connotations. Bunyan observes that 'Dark clouds bring waters, when the bright bring none' and adds a further metaphor from fishing:

> Yet Fish there be, that neither Hook, nor Line,
> Nor Snare, nor Net, nor engin can make thine:
> They must be grop'd for, and be tickled too,
> Or they will not be catcht, what e're you do.

Both authors assume that they have access to an audience prepared to undertake what is essentially an energetic form of reading, in which the reader's critical abilities are constantly brought into play by a desire to know and understand. The very labour of working things out is a part of the pleasure. Nor is that 'working out' simply clue-spotting, as with the *roman à clef* or fable, but an imaginative exercise in perceiving connections vertically and horizontally: vertically to significances outside the work, and horizontally to objects and events within it.

A phrase like 'significance outside the work' clearly begs questions. There is a very real sense in which significance, to exist, has to be in the work. Yet meaning may in the first instance be generated in the reader's mind by the work, and still be felt to have a close connection with beliefs or values independent of it. Medieval and renaissance allegories, and indeed most allegories until the eighteenth century, consistently both embody and point towards a system or metaphysic beyond the action and the reader. They are not exhortations to follow rigidly conceived norms of conduct and behaviour, but they do pose and analyse particular moral problems in relation to a general foundation of ethical judgments. The didacticism rests on collective values assumed to exist in the world as well as in the writer's imagination, even if conveyed in the literary work through the experiences of individuals and a unique pattern of images. The substance of the allegory could be seen as answering questions posed outside the work, and an enquiry into their validity: 'What should I do to ... inherit eternal life? attain a virtuous and noble life? become a true and happy lover? retain sanity in a confusing and threatening world?' Such exploratory didacticism will obviously be affected by the moral and imaginative commonplaces of the writer's society, and allegories often share qualities with straight instructional or theoretical works written at the same period. Langland uses materials and methods which also occur in medieval sermons, in books of private devotion, and in the *Artes Moriendi*; *Le Roman de la Rose* contains much that derives from the Ovidian tradition of advice on amorous behaviour, expressed most influentially in the *De Arte Honeste Amandi* of Andreas Capellanus; Spenser concerns himself with problems treated in the courtesy books of the Renaissance; Joseph K. confronts situations which reveal Kafka's awareness of questions in contemporary psychology and philosophy. Even *The Rape of the Lock*, a kind of one-dimensional allegory mid-way between total allegory and the fable or *roman à clef*, implicitly contrasts the silliness of Belinda's world with Augustan ideals of behaviour: 'And trust me, Dear! Good Humour can prevail,/When Airs, and Flights, and Screams, and Scolding fail.' The sentiment is an ironic version of something from a book of etiquette or of 'Advice to a Young Lady'.

In earlier allegories individual protagonists encounter monstrous, fabulous, and supernatural agencies all the time, but the significance of these encounters is a public one, the values those of Christianity, or a Christian aristocracy, or the commonplaces of an erotic convention, expressed in terms of the remote and extraordinary. This process is reversed in modern allegories (Kafka's two major works, for example) where protagonists endure commonplace, naturalistically presented experiences, but both meaning and value are recognized as internal or personal. The collective values are precisely those that threaten or obstruct the individual, and the significance of the action is often an assertion of solipsism against these. The primacy, and consequently isolation, of the individual is explored and articulated in terms of commonplace experience, and the action appears inconsequential because this experience is baffling : alienation is a central concept in modern allegories, though obviously this is to label a complex process rather crudely.

Allegory is a mode that undergoes many transformations in the course of its history, transformations so radical that they cannot be accounted for solely in literary critical terms (my final section will attempt some tentative historical and cultural explanations). Allegorical writing, like other kinds, changes because the material it seeks to analyse is changed – the world and society or, more precisely, people's knowledge and perception of them. More importantly for the argument here, its procedures are reversed, and reversed because the existence of real value independent of the individual becomes at least questionable. Far from endorsing the conventions and norms of established society, the mode increasingly criticizes, satirizes, and finally rejects them. It is true that *La Divina Commedia* contains scathing attacks on thirteenth-century Italian society, but these attacks occur in the context of a celestial vision : anger at human irrationality and corruption is balanced by the revelation of divine charity ordering the cosmos. Such a balance is almost always absent from modern allegories.

Satire risks movement towards despair, tragedy, nihilism (by contrast Dante's poem is a *commedia*); in satire it is undesirable that moral judgments should be elusive. Many modern allegories (such as those of Kafka, the brothers Čapek, or Orwell) are closer to satire in effect, if not always in tone, than are the earlier allegories. They are more negative – concerned to show what is wrong, or evil, or hostile rather than what is good or beneficent – and also tend to allow the reader rather less liberty of interpretation and possible application. The earlier function of allegory as a book of wisdom or instruction diminishes under pressure of subversive objectives, and a moral decisiveness has a formal correlative in the use of the fable, notoriously a vehicle for simple moralizations.

Readers of Orwell's *Animal Farm* and *1984* might well feel that the differences between these books and *The Faerie Queene* or its medieval predecessors are too great to allow them all to be called allegories. The animal fable and the futuristic dystopia resemble *The Faerie Queene* and *La Divina Commedia* in being clearly not realistic and entailing a high proportion of fantasy: pigs do not walk on their hind-legs, horses and sheep do not build windmills, governments – as yet – do not have telescreens in every individual's home. The fantasy exists to suggest serious secondary meanings, as in earlier allegories, and yet despite similarities the experience of reading Spenser and of reading Orwell remains very different – and not simply because one is distant in time. The problem here is that the reader is confronted with allegories cast in the form of fable or novel, and with those cast in other narrative forms such as the Christian journey of the soul or the chivalric Romance: i.e. with allegories that require to be *read* in different ways. The relationship between author and reader is different, as are the expectations the author has of his reader.

In reading about Artegall we are expected to interpret selectively all the time, since we need not only to generalize from Artegall to 'Justice' but thence to all the possible manifestations of justice. By contrast the morality of *Animal Farm* and *1984* is simple and consistent, and the narrative correspondingly easy to interpret. Napoleon the pig stands for an actual historical person, Stalin. Once that connection is made the reader is free to see Stalin as a type of all dictators, but in reading *Animal Farm* the connection between the fictional and incredible pig and the historical dictator is the important one. The fictional Artegall refers not to another concrete entity, but to an abstraction, a universal, which has never existed as an entity. *1984* is not a fable in the way that *Animal Farm* is, but it too requires a movement between fiction and history and between incredibility and probability. Winston Smith's collapse under torture, his total reconciliation to life in Oceania, and his acceptance of Big Brother as not merely credible but *lovable*, provoke a sharply negative reaction. The reaction combines belief that such things are morally incredible with the awareness that they are historically and technologically possible. The narrative inspires strong distaste for certain political and technological tendencies in advanced industrial societies by making us fear their potential outcome. The future dystopia is an allegory of tendencies at work in the present, an expression of their moral teleology. In reading Spenser or Bunyan or Langland the question 'Could this happen?' is entirely malapropos, because the didactic purpose is not historical awareness but individual enlightenment and subsequent action. It relates to shared values, but is personal and spiritual in its application rather than collective.

This may appear to contradict the claim made earlier that allegories before the eighteenth century usually relate to some system or metaphysic that is collective rather than personal in its origins. Certainly, both *The Pilgrim's Progress* and *Piers Plowman* are concerned precisely with collective values: Christianity and the state of Christian society. But in both the starting point is the question 'How may I save my soul?' and the action finds some kind of answer to that by showing what happens to an individual. Continuous interpretation results in the awareness of a hierarchy of value. This hierarchy may be rejected, but it is rejected by the reader for his own reasons, usually because the metaphysical implications are unacceptable. It is possible to conclude that the Heavenly City is not desirable, but not that Christian (or Bunyan) did not desire it, or that they thought it was unattainable. Courtesy may appear to any individual reader as a piece of aristocratic humbug, but we cannot think that it was humbug for Spenser, his readers, or for Calidore.

All the earlier allegories require constant interpretation and an imagination prepared to understand subtle gradations of value. Orwell's two books, and many modern allegories, require a single act of translation (fiction to history for example) and then can be read as straight narratives whose moral significance is obvious. Indeed, without that clearly delimited act of translation they lose half their force. Of course, even if the degree of interpretative activity demanded of readers is less in modern works, they share basic forms and objectives with earlier ones: an obvious point of comparison is that they are analyses of society in which certain characters and institutions play representative roles. The idea of the élite in *1984* operates in ways similar to that of the papacy or the curia in Dante's vision. We never have absolute freedom in reading allegory: if it takes less effort to understand the allegorical meaning of *1984*, it still cannot be understood as meaning anything whatsoever; the detailed local interpretation asked of us by Spenser does not absolve us from remembering the large-scale imaginative and moral significances. The more overtly didactic allegories are also those where the validity of some collective morality is most confidently asserted, and we might expect that these would leave us with least room for manœuvre. Paradoxically, this isn't the case: the individual reader's freedom is greater with them than with modern allegories where the subject is so often the frustration of the individual. The wider the range of possibilities in understanding an allegorical event, the greater the effort of selection. But that effort guarantees our freedom both in reading and in applying what we read to how we might act.

Two things make it difficult for modern writers to demand without irony this effort from their readers. Firstly, the expenditure of energy is ultimately justified by moral purpose, and if a writer cannot presume to be didactic then neither can he assume freely that his readers will be prepared to sweat over his work. Secondly, esoteric meanings are in a sense undemocratic: they cannot by definition be easily accessible or obviously relevant. Moreover, allegory is not only undemocratic but authoritarian in that its doubleness is the doubleness of action and implied commentary upon it. In some cases the commentary is explicit, as in *La Divina Commedia*, where both Virgil and Beatrice explain the action to the poet as it occurs. Northrop Frye makes the acute suggestion that this is one of the reasons why critics dislike allegory: they are prejudiced against it because 'continuous allegory prescribes the direction of [the critic's] commentary, and so restricts its freedom' (*Anatomy*, p.90). The idea that there are as many ways of reading a work of literature as there are readers is anathema to allegory.

For these reasons, and others to be discussed later, when modern authors do use allegorical methods they do so in nervous or deliberately ironic ways. Nabokov parodies an exegetical approach in *Pale Fire*, where commentary upon an insipid piece of verse is the narrative itself. The elaborate mock-picaresque of John Barth's *Giles Goat-Boy* and *The Sot-Weed Factor* operates in much the same way as a genuine allegory, but the secondary meanings are contained within the domain of purely literary response. This is also partly true of *Ulysses*, where awareness of the literary models parodied by Joyce is an important element in finding out what is happening and what it means. Borges constructs an imaginary universe through the fiction of academic sleuth-work on a rare article and unique edition; Pynchon constructs a secret society which dates from the seventeenth century and can only be discovered through arcane scholarship and courageous detective work. But *Pale Fire*, Borges's *Tlön, Uqbar, Orbis Tertius*, Pynchon's *Crying of Lot Forty-Nine*, are jokes. Beautiful jokes, but essentially burlesques of allegory and its methods, and of the notion that there is an irreducible core of meaning in any book. This attitude towards allegory, and towards its methods and the view of the world that its methods assume, is not exclusively to be found in twentieth-century authors. Swift's impatience with ideas and values not accessible to 'commune sence' is at least part of the impulse behind *A Tale of a Tub* and its elaborate prefaces.

The claim of the title page that *A Tale of a Tub* is 'Written for the Universal Improvement of Mankind' mocks moralistic and didactic intentions. The attempt to 'have a thorough comprehension of an author's thoughts' becomes ludicrous when Swift asserts in 'The Author's Preface' that the way to achieve this is for the reader to put himself

> into the circumstances and postures of life, that the writer
> was in upon every important passage, as it flowed from his
> pen : for this will introduce a parity, and a strict correspondance
> of ideas, between the reader and the author.

In the particular context of *A Tale of a Tub*, 'it will be absolutely impossible for the candid peruser to go along with me in a great many bright passages' unless he is in bed in a garret, starving, and penurious. The pursuit of allegorical meaning is deflated by the idea of going about it literally, as it is also in the earlier passage in 'The Author's Preface' giving the supposed circumstances in which the work was written.

> At a grand committee some days ago, this important discovery
> was made by a certain curious and refined observer – that
> seamen have a custom, when they meet a whale, to fling him
> out an empty tub by way of amusement, to divert him from
> laying violent hands upon the ship. This parable was
> immediately mythologised; the whale was interpreted to be
> Hobbes' *Leviathan*, which tosses and plays with all schemes of
> religion and government, whereof a great many are hollow,
> and dry, and empty, and noisy, and wooden, and given to
> rotation : this is the leviathan, whence the terrible wits of

our age are said to borrow their weapons. The ship is easily
understood to be its old antitype, the commonwealth. But how
to analyse the tub, was a matter of difficulty; when, after long
enquiry and debate, the literal meaning was preserved; and it
was decreed that, in order to prevent these leviathans from
tossing and sporting with the commonwealth, which of itself
is too apt to fluctuate, they should be diverted from that game
by a *Tale of a Tub*.

The meaning of the barrel is a barrel, but the work itself is *like* a
barrel, and aimed at those the work condemns, the wits. Its
function is not to carry meaning, to contain anything, but to divert
– in the sense of 'to entertain' and 'to deflect'. Distrust of enigma
and all allegorical methods as involving élitist assumptions is also
obvious in Section I of *A Tale of a Tub*. Whoever wants to be
heard in a crowd must climb 'till he has exalted himself to a
certain degree of altitude above them . . . . To this end, the philosopher's way, in all ages, has been by erecting certain edifices in the
air'. Again, a literal interpretation of 'edifices' (as pulpits, ladders,
and movable stages) mocks those writers whose meanings are difficult of access, for they 'have often been out of sight, and ever out of
hearing.' Truth becomes a tone of voice, a way of looking, a turn
of phrase, rather than an object of statement in the work. *A Tale
of a Tub* is a deliberate parody of the allegorical method, a brilliant
palimpsest of irony. The different levels of parody and irony offer
several perspectives upon the minimal narrative and on the work
as a whole, and themselves parody the idea of levels of meaning –
such as those discovered in sacred texts by medieval exegetes. The
reader needs to be alert to the moment at which a new perspective
has displaced an earlier one, even as he needs to interpret continuously and selectively in earlier allegories.

   A medieval allegorist, or Spenser, or Bunyan, could assume that
the energy expended in discovering meaning was justified, because
it could lead to an awareness of values worthy of pursuit. Swift, as
a satirist, does not. Satire suggests what kind of behaviour is stupid
or despicable, what ideas are contemptible or risible; allegory does
so only in passing. In the first case effort is directed towards the
rejection of what is valueless, in the second toward the discovery of
value. Positive values may be implied in satire by the presentation
of their opposites, but in allegory the metaphysical goals are

almost always explicitly expressed in some object or event in the narrative.

The prefaces to *Gulliver's Travels* are also parodic of earlier allegorists' assumptions about and invitations to their readers, though the work itself is not as profoundly ironic as *A Tale of a Tub*. Swift destroys the possibility of the book being read merely as fantastic invention or as straight reportage by the strenuous assertions that there is nothing to interpret – any reader is made suspicious. The poker-faced refusal to indicate secondary meanings is appropriate to the satirical, fabling side of allegory. Langland's explicitly political allegory in the Prologue to *Piers Plowman*, that of the rats' unsuccessful attempt to bell the cat, which shows the folly of the commons' attempts to curb royal power, ends on the same note:

> What this dream means guess for yourselves, you who are carefree, for I dare not, by dear God in heaven.
>
> (Prologue ll. 208-9)

When the Friars are attacked as an order particularly responsible for corrupting the institutions of the Church, the same point is made by the Dreamer: 'if I *dared* ... among men show forth this dream' (Passus XI 86). The inhibition here is political, as it is to a lesser extent in Swift's more sophisticated 'Letter from Captain Gulliver'. 'Cousin Sympson', the publisher, is reported as being afraid of giving offence because 'people in power were very watchful over the press; and apt not only to interpret, but to punish everything which looked like an innuendo'. The refusal to interpret or the assertion that there is nothing to interpret are both provocative; they are as much invitations to the reader as Bunyan's imperious demands.

Literature in which significances are not 'Plaine shewen' is a kind of club for the initiated, flattering their intelligence by suggesting that they have the necessary interpretative skill (as in *Pale Fire* or *A Tale of a Tub*). It often happens that readers or authors who feel that the concealment of moral or intellectual or spiritual truth under surface obscurity is undesirably exclusive will be tolerant of the concealment of political or satirical truth. Sympathy for the use of allegory for political purposes is understandable, since obliqueness equals security. Subterfuge becomes the only way of setting out certain values, if these values are

regarded as subversive by those in power. Even in an early discussion of allegorical figures by Puttenham (*The Arte of English
Poesie*, Book III xviii), there are constant allusions to the subversive
potential of the mode. The 'drie mocke', the 'merry scoffe', the
'privy nippe', the 'loud lier' (*ironia, asteismus, charientismus, hyper-
bole*), all hold 'somewhat of the dissembler, by reason of a secret
intent not appearing by the words, as when we go about the bush,
and will not in one or a few words expresse that thing which we
desire to have knowen, but do chose rather to do it by many words'.
The last quotation comes from the discussion of *periphrasis*, but
Puttenham emphasizes the dissembling nature of all the figures; and
all allegory is to a considerable degree periphrastic.

Obscurity of surface in political allegory (where it is usually
seen as permissible) and in moral or intellectual allegory (where
it may be regarded with suspicion as élitist) are equally related to
the desire to safeguard allegorical meaning. From this desire derives
also the commonplace device of presenting the allegory as a dream
or vision (the *meteles* of Langland), or the fiction that it occurs in
a manuscript discovered by the author, or by now beyond his
control (as with *Gulliver's Travels*). James Hogg takes such dis-
tancing devices to the extreme in *The Private Memoirs and
Confessions of a Justified Sinner*. Appended to the text of the
Memoirs is an account of the finding of the Sinner's body, in a letter
to *Blackwood's Magazine* for August 1823. The intrigued 'Editor'
shows this letter, signed 'James Hogg', to a friend who comments
that 'Hogg has imposed as ingenious lies on the public ere now'.
Curious to discover the circumstances of this bizarre death, the
Editor sets out for Thirlestane, and enquires of James Hogg
(presented as a shepherd selling his sheep at the sheep-fair) where
he can find the grave mentioned in the letter. 'Hogg' replies: 'Od
bless ye, lad! I hae ither matters to mind .... I hae mair ado than I
can manage the day, foreby ganging to houk up hunder-year-auld
banes.' But the 'Editor' goes to the grave, disinters the body again,
and finds on it the manuscript containing this 'religious PARABLE,
showing the dreadful danger of self-righteousness'. This intricate
fiction for separating the author from his work is not identical
with the methods used by mainstream allegorists, since it is compounded by a somewhat Gothic taste for the fantastic in the guise
of the actual. But it is again provocative, and serves to confer on
the *Memoirs* themselves a more potent kind of significance. It is

also reminiscent of the way in which medieval authors write themselves into their allegories in the personae of 'the Dreamer' or 'the
Poet'.

By simulating detachment and lack of control the author acts
out irresponsibility for the substance of the work and places
responsibility for the meaning to be derived from it on the reader.
This procedure can be defensive – as in the case of allegories
aiming at political subversion – and serve to protect the author as
much as his meaning. But all modern allegories, even those which
are not political, either demand fewer and less complex acts of
interpretation of their readers, or make the demand ironically.
Ironically, because the assumptions that there is 'a meaning'
independent of the vagaries of readers' comparative judgments, and
that it has practical consequences, are viewed with scepticism.

Writers like Langland, Spenser, or Bunyan have a rationale
which contrasts with this scepticism. Their presumption that the
reader will be prepared not merely to tolerate but to engage with
the enigmas and obscurities and metaphors of allegory rests on
confidence in its moral function. Whereas in their books the process
of finding things out is justified by what hero and reader discover,
in reading Kafka or Melville that process is not only self-validating
but even leads to a denial that there is anything to find out: the
end justifies the means versus there is no end but the means. In
earlier allegories the intellectual exercise gives pleasure in itself
but is also a preparation for the point at which the reader applies
what he reads to how he acts. Since it is never easy to perceive
what is good or bad, the elusiveness of the abstractions in the
allegory makes us exercise faculties of judgment needed to deal
with the manifestations of these abstractions in our own experience.
Reading a difficult allegory is intellectually and imaginatively useful
where simple allegory ('good discipline deliuered plainly') is effective in only the most admonitory and unanalytic way. Moreover,
the potentially restrictive nature of allegory is alleviated by the
act of continuous detailed interpretation, since that creates a feeling
of responsibility in the reader, and of control over his own imaginative experience.

All such arguments in defence of allegory and of the obligations
it imposes on its audience are secondary to the belief that it is
particularly suited to the transmission of kinds of truth that would

resist other methods of expression. It is with this view of allegory that the next section will concern itself.

2 Coherence, fragmentation, and system

Allegory presupposes readers assiduous in interpreting (rather than simply following or responding to) a narrative. This emphatically does not imply that interpretation is reductive: the greatest allegories are intransigent and elusive not simply for defensive reasons such as political caution but because they are concerned with a highly complex kind of truth, a matter of relationships and process rather than statement. The elusiveness of truth is a measure of its value, as in Donne's Satyre III, 'Kinde pitty chokes my spleene':

> On a huge hill,
> Cragged, and steep, Truth stands, and hee that will
> Reach her, about must, and about must goe;
> And what the hills suddennes resists, winne so;
>
> (79-82)

The greater the value of what the allegory signifies, the more it 'resists', and difficulty of reading protects it from casual and therefore falsifying interpretation. Writers of allegory conceive of truth as in some degree hermetic, too complex to be rendered in baldly prescriptive or descriptive language. The allegorical action is not a paraphrase of something capable of alternative expression.

The heart of all allegories is a focus of multiple interpretations rather than *a* meaning, but by no means all allegories are equally confident about the possibility and purposes of interpretation. Older allegories assume that the world as well as the work is legible, susceptible to being 'read'. They move through the intricacies of system towards an order that assumes moral coherence, and break down concepts into components in the interests of clarity and ultimate unification. Their coherence is connected with a sense of continuity: continuity between particular experience and general philosophic statements, between individuals and groups, between past, present, and future. Encyclopaedism reflects confidence in the wholeness and perspicuousness of the world. In modern allegories digression is not an excursion into another part of the same coherent system, but parodic or even futile, a reflection of the essential fragmentation of the universe and our intellectual relationship with it.

Again, while all allegory has affinities with myth (affinities to be discussed later in this section) there is a divergence between the ways in which mythological allusion functions in Spenser, and in Melville or Kafka. Myth, like allegory, is concerned with a complex and coherent system of explanation. It attempts to offer means by which we can interpret our relationship to the past, to the forces operating in the psyche, and to the facts and processes of the world around us. The essential difference is that myth is in an important sense pre-literary while allegory is a literary mode that borrows from myth, subordinating it to its own purposes. And the purposes which it serves in earlier allegories are distinct from those it serves in more modern ones: while Spenser uses the figure of Adonis to help interpretation of complex ideas about love and time and regeneration, Melville twists the myth of Narcissus and makes it suggest that the attempt to interpret is madness and self-destruction as much as the pursuit of wisdom.

> And still deeper the meaning of that story of Narcissus,
> who because he could not grasp the tormenting, mild image
> he saw in the fountain, plunged into it and was drowned.
> But that same image, we ourselves see in all rivers and oceans.
> It is the image of the ungraspable phantom of life; and this
> is the key to it all.
>
> (*Moby Dick*, Chapter 1, p.95)

Sidney's *An Apology for Poetry* contains many observations that are particularly applicable to allegory and its methods, and among them the notion that the poet achieves something more illuminating, and thus more profoundly moral, than either the historian or the philosopher. The knowledge of the philosopher

> standeth so upon the abstract and general, that happy is that man who may understand him, and more happy that can apply what he doth understand.
>
> (*An Apology for Poetry*, p.107)

The historian, on the other hand,

> wanting the precept, is so tied, not to what should be but to what is, to the particular truth of things, and not to the

general reason of things, that his example draweth no necessary consequence, and therefore a less fruitful doctrine.

(ibid., p.107)

But the poet 'coupleth the general notion with the particular example' and

> yieldeth to the powers of the mind an image of that whereof
> the philosopher bestoweth but a wordish description, which
> doth neither strike, pierce, nor possess the sight of the soul. . . .

(ibid., p.107)

In the letter in which Spenser expounds his purpose in writing *The Faerie Queen* there is a passage which parallels Sidney's claim that poetry is more analytic than history:

> For an Historiographer discourseth of affayres orderly as they
> were donne . . . but a Poet thrusteth into the middest, euen
> where it most concerneth him, and there recoursing to the
> thinges forepaste, and diuining of things to come, maketh
> a pleasing Analysis of all.

(*Works*, p.408)

Most medieval and renaissance allegories move between philosophy and history; their authors use particular examples to express the 'general reason of things', and also draw much of their material from sacred and secular history and from earlier literature ('thinges forepaste'). This multiplicity of sources is one of the factors that give the analytic content of allegory its power, making its images more striking than straightforward description or narrative exposition.

The object of 'pleasing Analysis' is some perceived order or pattern in the world or (in earlier allegories) in the cosmos. The reader is presumed to derive pleasure and potential benefit from interpreting the work since he can thus extrapolate from it values which are relevant to understanding the material world and his particular situation. What he interprets, the allegory itself, is also a dramatically presented anatomy of a highly structured view of reality. Allegory is always profoundly aware of system; the belief that there is one supreme ordering of the cosmos, of which certain social or civic systems are only a reflection, frequently underlies the action. This is very clear in the *La Divina Commedia*, *Piers Plowman*, and *The Faerie Queene*. Even Kafka's works centre on the conception of system – usually one that frustrates the hero because his knowledge of it is necessarily partial, and its metaphysical significance obscure.

One example of the kind of system or model found in earlier allegories occurs in Chaucer's allegorical dream-vision *The Parlement of Foules*. The first part of the poem is almost pure allegory, while the second presents the pairing of the birds on St Valentine's Day in the form of a more realistically conceived debate-poem. The view of order that underlies the poem is in part social, expressed in the mating of each of the birds with one of their own kind. The courtship of the formel eagle by the three royal tercels suggests that emotional assent is as important as social order, and that none of the birds has the right to a mate without her full consent:

> But natheles, in this condicioun
> Mot be the choys of everich that is heere,
> That she agre to his eleccioun,
> Whoso he be that shulde be hire feere.
> *(Parlement, 407-10)*

(*eleccioun* : choice; *feere* : companion, mate)

This social and emotional basis for the propriety of sexual unions is extended by the allusions to the *Somnium Scipionis* that open the poem, and by numerous references to another kind of ordering which underlies the hierarchy of the various birds. Chaucer begins by showing the poet reading the *Somnium*, in which Africanus appears to Scipio in a dream, and shows him the 'lytel erthe' seen from the heavens:

> And after shewede he hym the nyne speres,
> And after that the melodye herde he
> That cometh of thilke speres thryes thre,
> That welle is of musik and melodye
> In this world here, and cause of armonye.
> *(ibid., 59-63)*

(*speres* : spheres; *thilke* : those; *armonye* : harmony)

Africanus then comes to the poet in his own dream, and shows him a garden (the *hortus conclusus* which in different forms is central to so many allegories – the Garden of Mirth in *Le Roman de la*

Rose, the Garden of Adonis in *The Faerie Queene*). Above the two halves of the door into the garden are verses which suggest the contrary effects of love:
'Thorgh me men gon into that blisful place/Of hertes hele' and 'Thorgh me men gon .../Unto the mortal strokes of the spere'. But once in the garden these two poles of experience are held in balance.

> Of instruments of strenges in acord
> Herde I so pleye a ravyshyng swetnesse,
> That God, that makere is of al and lord,
> Ne herde nevere beter, as I gesse.
> Therwith a wynd, unnethe it myghte be lesse,
> Made in the leves grene a noyse softe
> Acordaunt to the foules song alofte.
>
> Th'air of that place so attempre was
> That nevere was ther grevaunce of hot ne cold;
> There wex ek every holsom spice and gras;
> Ne man may there waxe sek ne old;
> Yit was there joye more a thousandfold
> Than man can telle; ne nevere wolde it nyghte
> But ay cler day to any manes syghte.
>
> (*ibid.*, 197-210)

(*acord*: harmony; *unnethe*: unless; *attempre*: temperate; *wex*: grew; *wolde it*: was it, would be it; *manes*: man's)

The 'acord' between the music, the 'noyse softe' of the wind among the leaves, and the 'foules song alofte' is an echo of the celestial music, 'That welle is of musik and melodye/In this world here, and cause of armonye.' The relationship of the cosmic to the mundane is causative, and the hierarchical considerations governing the mating of the birds are validated by a metaphysical order: 'To every foul Nature yaf his make/By evene *acord*.' Nature acts in the poem as a good-natured arbiter for the birds, but is also connected with *natura naturans*, God in his creating aspect. She represents not nature as an observed phenomenon, but the laws of order and regeneration which govern the natural world, and which are here intimately connected with divine laws.

The conceptions underlying Chaucer's presentation of Nature are not however confined to the particular theology of a particular period. Even the Romantic poets at their least theological claim for nature an ordering as well as an ordered power. Wordsworth describes the 'immeasurable height/ Of woods decaying, never to be decayed./The stationary blasts of waterfalls' in the Simplon pass, as

> ... all like workings of one mind, the features
> Of the same face, blossoms upon one tree;
> Characters of the great Apocalypse,
> The types and symbols of Eternity
> Of first, and last, and midst, and without end.
>   (*The Prelude*, Book VI 624-6 and 636-40)

The order here is one seen in temporal terms, a kind of frozen order rather than a rhythmic one. It is awe-inspiring rather than reassuring. By contrast the landscape of the Lake District, more familiar and on a smaller scale, is a source of benevolent inspiration:

> ... virtue have the forms
> Perennial of the ancient hills . . . .
> The Spirit of Nature was upon me there;
> The soul of Beauty and enduring Life
> Vouchsafed her inspiration, and diffused ...
> Composure, and ennobling Harmony.
>   (*ibid.*, Book VII 756-7 and 766-71)

In a curious way this is semantically *more* allegorical than Chaucer, since the latter simply shows Nature as performing something, whereas Wordsworth gives it a 'Spirit', puts it in apposition to 'the soul of Beauty' (an apposition probably tautologous for a medieval poet), and then attributes to it the power to diffuse composure and ennobling harmony. Part of the problem is that direct dramatic personification, a literary commonplace in the fourteenth century, had become too artificial by the nineteenth century to be used with any ease. Wordsworth and other Romantic poets have often to resort to vagueness in order to express supposed connections between the physical and particular and the metaphysical and abstract. Nor of course is it simply that the techniques of earlier allegories had become discredited, but also that the confident world-view and collectively accesible model of reality that they expressed was no longer viable.

The simple narrative action of *The Parlement of Foules* is closer to debate poem than allegories such as *Le Roman de la Rose* and *Piers Plowman*, but its language reveals the preoccupation with order and metaphysical system which is so often a feature of allegories. The sensuous details of the garden, the 'attempre' air and the noise among the leaves, are pleasant in themselves; they are also pleasing in that they suggest that sensuous detail can be experienced and understood in terms of abstractions without any loss of vitality and complexity. Chaucer makes connections between two orders of reality and between two historically separate experiences, Scipio's and his own. The poet thus gains cosmic insights (and social and emotional ones, even though these appear to us as more like prejudices) via literary and historical means.

In *Piers Plowman* the satirical and critical impulses make it less easy to perceive any presentation of order in the world, at least in the world of man-made institutions. The satirist has always found much of his material in chaos and lawlessness, whether it is presented as an omnipotent deity triumphing over intellectual order, as at the end of *The Dunciad*, or as visual chaos and confusion, as in Hogarth's *Gin Lane* or Rowlandson's cartoons. In social chaos extremes of behaviour cause individuals to struggle with each other and with themselves, even as in Milton's description of material Chaos, 'where length, bredth, and height/And time and place are lost', the atoms fight 'endless warrs'. But Langland is not principally a satirist, and the Seven Deadly Sins or Lady Mede (Money) are objects of satirical attack because they violate not only a social order, but a metaphysical one; the passages concerning them are carefully contained within that part of the poem where the subject is precisely the absence of any organization. The problems confronting the Dreamer/Poet arise from an inability to see any kind of order and hierarchy in the world, and the questions that this makes him ask are the principal means by which new phases in the exposition are initiated.

It is worth spending some time on the allegorical action of *Piers Plowman*, because it is an allegory often accused of inconsistency and lack of organization. Yet it shows a very careful concern with systematization both in its literal and intellectual structures. The opening landscape of the vision is clearly organized: the Tower of Truth on a high hill to the east against the sun, beneath it a great dark gulf in which is the dungeon of Wrong, father of Falsehood, and between these two a great plain on which mankind hastens about, oblivious of what lies to either side. The structured polarities of this image anticipate some of the more important aspects of the system which underlies the rest of the poem. The fair woman clothed in linen who interprets this landscape for the Dreamer is Holichurch, the Church in its ideal rather than its institutional form. She functions dramatically in the same way as Philosophy in Boethius' *De Consolatione Philosophiae* or Virgil in *La Divina Commedia*: as an Expositor. The dialogue between her and the Dreamer provides in concentrated form a model for the allegorical action and its dominant objective. Having learnt the meaning of the Tower, the Dungeon, and the Plain, the Dreamer asks, 'How may I save my soul?' and is answered that he who performs all things in truth shall attain salvation. He protests that he has no natural knowledge ('kynde knowing') of truth and asks by what bodily faculty it may be apprehended, thus showing that he has already assumed an unduly narrow definition of 'natural'. Holichurch tells him that it is indeed a 'kynde knowing' that teaches the heart to love God and to avoid sin (the manifestation of which is love for one's neighbours), and that to act with love is to act as Truth itself, as God. The Dreamer's last question of Holichurch, How can the false be distinguished? initiates that part of the poem which treats most of the disorder and abuses of human society, and which is most exclusively satirical. Later, as he searches for some alternative to a world so clearly devoid of both Truth and Charity, his questions re-formulate those asked at the outset. The object of his search becomes 'Dowel', but since Do Well is that way of life which makes it possible to pass into eternal life, this is no more than an objectification of the query, How may I save my soul? The Dreamer is hurried from one instructor to another (as Gulliver from one country to another, or K. from one baffling experience to the next), but fails to gain clarification because he has not understood the hierarchy of values presented to him at the beginning by Holichurch.

His encounters with Thought, Wit (Intelligence), Wit's wife Study, her cousins Clergy (Learning) and Scripture, are all in a sense encounters with aspects of himself. This is suggested by physical similarities: The Dreamer is tall and thin, Thought seems to him 'a tall man, much like himself', Wit is 'long and lean', and Dame Study is also 'lean of face'. What is allegorized here is a mistaken fragmentation of the pursuit: the Dreamer is trying to learn the nature of Truth through various single faculties. In this Langland used the same method as de Lorris, Spenser, or Swift, that of separating out and objectifying aspects of a hero's character or experience in order to clarify the system he wanted to expound. And like Spenser's Redcrosse or Bunyan's Christian, it is only the vision of something absolutely outside his own experience that enables the Dreamer to break out of the limitations of isolated individual effort to a more valuable kind of action. In the case of the Dreamer, this vision is shown him by Kynde (Nature), who summons him to learn from the wonders of this world.

> And on a mountain called middle-earth, as I then thought,
> I was taken forth to know by examples and through each
> creature and species how to love my Creator. I saw the sun
> and the sea and the sand after, and where birds and beasts went
> with their mates ... but the thing that moved me most and
> changed my mind was that Reason rewarded and governed
> all beasts, save man and his mate.
>
> (XI 315-19 and 360-2)

This immense vision of the world (here necessarily much cut) and its reasonable balance is in direct contrast to the confused world of human experience and institutions which preceded the unsuccessful interrogations of Thought, Wit, Study, Clergy, and Scripture. It is from this vision that the Dreamer passes to a meeting with Ymagynatyf, who is able to set all these disparate authorities in some kind of harmonious relation, and to show their relevance to the pursuit of salvation. After another brief section, more dramatic and satirical, Anima is introduced as the next figure to address the hero directly in a helpfully expository way. She claims for herself the names of Life, Soul, Mind, Memory, Reason, Sense (the first name, since it is through the senses that perceiving intelligence, Wit, and cumulative intelligence, Wisdom, create all knowledge and skill), Conscience, Love, and Spirit. In short, all the fragmentations of the Dreamer's mind and experience, and those of the action of the poem, are re-united in a single figure. It is Anima who indicates that it is Piers the Ploughman who alone can help the Dreamer to a true perception of Charity, and who equates Piers with Christ. This is the last stage of preparation necessary for the final journey to the vision of the Crucifixion and the Harrowing of Hell, mythic events by which the metaphysical order is finally imposed upon the disorder of sin, upon the chaos of the great plain of mankind analysed in the early stages of the poem.

Langland is concerned with two kinds of order and system, the first cosmic and hieratic, extending from Truth and Charity to Falsehood and Cupidity, and the second a more horizontal kind which distinguishes the various faculties of the mind and different modes of experience. The poem is also organized in purely formal ways by the several dream units, and by imagery such as the agrarian kind which centres on the Christ-Ploughman. For example, 'heathen', in the general sense of one not knowing truth rather than the racialist sense given it in the nineteenth century, is given an etymology from 'heath'.

> Hethene is to mene after heth . and untiled erthe
> As in wilde wildernesse . wexeth wilde bestes
> Rude and unreasonable.

> ('Heathen' has the same sort of meaning as heath, untiled earth, as in the wild wilderness beasts became rough and unreasonable.)

The pursuit of truth is thus paralleled by the cultivation of land – to understand something of the nature of truth it is necessary to order the mind and the imagination.

It would be possible to perform the same kind of analysis on *La Divina Commedia*, but with that poem the concern for structure is more overt and strikes most readers forcibly. The detailed geography of the Poet's journey, the carefully organized symbolism of the poem, its numerical structures, the placing of historical and mythical figures within a moral scale, all contribute to the presentation of a vision supremely comprehensive and ordered. It is analogous, as many of its critics have observed, to those great intellectual documents of the Middle Ages, the *Summae*. Spenser and Langland, as much as Dante, offer a 'pleasing Analysis', despite differences in the imaginative terms in which it is expressed. Dante's terms are overtly political and historical as well as Christian and philosophical; Spenser's are romantic, chivalric, and pastoral; while Langland's are psychological, epistemological, apocalyptic, and popular. In all three works the shape of the allegorical narrative is directed by some scheme of values. This scheme or system, while almost independent of the action, controls its overall struc-

ture and determines the relationship between the particular incidents. But in none of these works is it an exclusive or limiting
system, since all of them include a wealth of material from history,
philosophy, the satirical observation of contemporary life, and a
variety of intellectual disciplines we would now consider as at best
marginal to literature. One of the great advantages of allegory is
that it can contain or analyse without irrelevance such a range of
experience.

The preceding section contains the implicit assumption that
allegory thrives on the inclusion of a wide range of material, and
with pre-eighteenth-century allegories it is permissible to assume
that. The encyclopaedic humanism of the twelfth century, which
was so important for the intellectual history of the next three
centuries, affected allegories as much as it did ecclesiastical art and
theology. Allegories, so often concerned with rendering a whole
world through a single perspective, even if only temporarily, do
stand to benefit from the belief that science, natural history,
medicine, mathematics, chemistry, alchemy, music, theology,
poetry, grammar, and the visual arts, are all intimately connected.
Moreover, it was one of the more important tenets of the intellectual revolution of the twelfth century that man had an unlimited
capacity for knowledge. Alone among the creatures of the universe
he was capable of comprehending it, and with the aid of reason
could attain to at least intellectual understanding of the perfection
that the creation had initially possessed. This understanding was a
vital element in the regeneration of himself and his world, since one
of the consequences of the Fall was ignorance, and only by
attempts to eradicate that branch of sin could man begin his moral
restoration. Such ideas were also consequential for the development
of allegory, since they redeem intellectual diversity from the charge
of dilettantism. A work that was comprehensive was considered a
more effective moral instrument than one which was carefully
delimited. Thus writings like Bernard Silvestris's *De Universitate
Mundi*, and Alain de Lille's *De Planctu Naturae* or *Anticlaudianus*,
range confidently over universal history, geography, cosmology,
the seven liberal arts, and sex. Characters such as Noys (the Divine
Intellect), Natura, and Genius (who reappears in Gower's *Confessio
Amantis*, *Le Roman de la Rose*, and in Spenser's Garden of Adonis),
provide a framework of allegorical action within which this diverse
material is harmonized.

The recurrent figure of the world as Mirror or Book suggests the omnipresence of this kind of encyclopaedism. For Alain de Lille, the entire world is a sign of man's condition:

> Omnis mundi creatura
> Quasi liber et pictura
>   Nobis est in speculum.

(All creation, like a book or picture, is a mirror to us.)

In the *Dies Irae* Thomas of Celano uses the same figure:

> Liber scriptus proferetur
> In quo totum continetur,
> Unde mundus judicetur.

(The written book will be brought forward, in which is contained everything by which the world will be judged.)

If this kind of book is made by God, it is still possible that an individual can mirror God's activity by making a book which is, comparatively speaking, as comprehensive. The image of the world as book survives into the seventeenth century, but thereafter becomes less and less common. Goethe commented in *Maxims and Reflections* that

> Shakespeare is rich in wonderful tropes which stem from personified concepts and which would not suit us at all, but which in him are perfectly in place because in his time all art was dominated by allegory. ... he finds images where we would not go for them, for example in the book.
>
> (quoted in Curtius, p.303)

In Frances Quarles's *Emblems* (1655) the figure is also used:

> The world's a book in folio, printed all
> With God's great works in letters capital:
> Each creature is a page; and each effect
> A fair character, void of all defect.
>
> (*ibid.*, p.323)

Thereafter, the increasing multiplication and separation of speculative modes makes the use of the figure less probable; not even a folio could contain a picture of the universe.

Galileo wrote of the book of the universe lying open but illegible to most men: illegible because they did not understand the language in which it was written, a mathematical language of triangles, circles and squares. This comment marks a great change, the beginning of the fragmentation of the intellectual world and the dividing up of the imaginative universalism available to Alain de Lille, Dante, Langland, or Spenser. The fragmentation is suggested by the way in which attitudes to digression change. Swift is contemptuous of those who do not stick to the point in *A Tale of a Tub*, and both he and the very different Sterne use digression in parodic or highly artificial ways (whether it is upon Madness or a Nose). It could perhaps be argued that Sterne offers some 'allegorical' figure for the randomly associative nature of human thought; whether or not this is true, his attitude to digression is still highly self-conscious. By contrast, the idea of digression as necessarily boring or irritating or artficial is absent from medieval literature; 'amplification' or 'embellishment' were the terms used for excursions into subject matter now regarded as separate from literature.

This comparison perhaps indicates some of the differences in imaginative freedoms which earlier and later writers enjoyed, among them the would-be writers of allegory. Since the Enlightenment, the Encyclopaedia has become a book written by no single person, and certainly not intended to be read by anyone: it is an exercise in compilation and organization rather than understanding. (Hugh Kenner in *The Pound Era* (1972) calls the *New English Dictionary* the epic of the nineteenth century.) This does not seem a matter of the transformation of authorial taste, since the immense range of straight information contained in the novels of nineteenth-century authors such as Balzac, Dickens, or Flaubert suggests that some of the inclusiveness of *La Divina Commedia* continued to constitute a valid goal for writers. Flaubert of course provided the comic heroes of our time in Bouvard and Pécuchet. Their battle is with fragmented, undigested knowledge such as might be derived from a Larousse, and which lacks any kind of coherence. The heroes of modern allegories, unlike those of an earlier period, similarly confront a universe which is fragmented and devoid of overall significance and purpose. The attempt to gain comprehensive knowledge, the belief that it is relevant to the human situation, and the inclusion of it in a literary work as a valuable moral instrument, can all only seem comic.

In the desire to express order in the world through narrative comprehensive but systematic, allegory shows obvious affinities with myth. The latter controls and explains a wide range of cosmic, psychological and historical phenomena by imposing a continuous narrative, and attributing particular powers to particular figures in that narrative. Despite certain differences, such as that Classical and Judaeo-Christian mythology are anthropomorphic, while other mythologies use non-human agents extensively, all myth could be seen as an attempt to offer collectively acceptable explanation via some system of analogies. It is true that not all myths function equally as a vehicle for inherited belief about the historical past and the structure of the cosmos, or as explanation of that inheritance, nor indeed are particular myths always expressed in identical narrative forms. None the less, all these elements exist in varying proportions in myth, and they are elements also to be found in allegory. Anthropologists who have worked extensively in the study of mythologies, notably Lévi-Strauss, have suggested that widely separated myths may exhibit similar structures because these structures are the product of some universal primitive logic attempting to reconcile contradictions between unconscious wishes and conscious experience. Similarly, a recent critic of medieval allegories, Paul Piehler, has observed that many earlier allegories are frequently concerned with the dialectic between rationality and other pre-rational thoughts and beliefs.

Despite the connections and similarities, the distinction between allegory and myth is that whereas the latter attempts to explain a scarcely known past, allegory uses that past as a stylistic device to criticize and expound the present, even if that present takes a fictional form. Allegory is always conscious; the writer knows what he is doing and why he is doing it. Myth cannot be conscious and invented, otherwise it would lose its sacred value, its quality of being divinely true. Some comments by a recent critic of Lévi-Strauss are relevant here.

> ... the special quality of myth is not that it is false but that it is divinely true for those who believe, but fairy-tale for those who do not. The distinction that history is true and myth is false is quite arbitrary. Nearly all human societies possess a corpus of tradition about their own past.
>
> (Edmund Leach, *Lévi-Strauss*, p.54)

Both forms exhibit essentially 'conservative' tendencies, but whereas myth is in many societies the sole means by which the past is preserved, the allegorist is using a corpus of tradition available else-where. He does this to effect understanding of the abstractions which he believes controls equally 'thinges forepaste' and 'the diuining of thinges to come'. The difference between a mythological deity and an abstraction is that the events initiated by the former can be divinely true, while those initiated by the latter can only be intellectually or imaginatively 'true'. Medieval allegories which include divine persons or events seem to contradict this. But the divine occurs in the context of something else, namely a literary work. In *Piers Plowman* the vision of the Harrowing of Hell is a vision, a re-enactment; its importance in that work is that it influences the Dreamer, and our understanding of the Dreamer's experience which form the narrative of the poem.

The operation of personified universals often approximates to those of deities, and in this allegory may be seen as the inheritor of myth, and as fulfilling similar psychological needs. In Western culture, allegory develops after the spread of Christianity, the monotheistic mythology of which includes no pantheon of gods and goddesses, and is essentially an historical, a temporal myth. Coleridge, noting the absence of narrative and epic allegories at the classical period, attributes this to the multiplicity of their gods and goddesses. 'Of a people who raised altars to fever, to sport, to fright, etc., it is impossible to determine how far they meant a personal power or a personification of a power' (quoted in Alpers, p.140). He goes on to observe that 'The most beautiful allegory ever composed, "The Tale of Cupid and Psyche"' and 'the first allegory completely modern in its form ... the *Psychomachia* or *Battle of the Soul* by Prudentius' are both subsequent to the spread of Christianity; this fact suggests

> both the origin and nature of narrative allegory, as a substitute
> for the mythological imagery of polytheism, and differing
> from it only in the more obvious and intentional distinction
> of the sense from the symbol, and the known unreality of the
> latter—so as to be a kind of intermediate step between actual
> persons and mere personifications.
>
> (*ibid.*, p.140)

This historical position of allegory as the inheritor of myth has interesting effects upon the way in which personifications are presented.

Spenser often emphasizes the representative nature of his characters until they become solely an abstraction. In Book III, Malbecco's wife Hellenore is abducted by Paridell with her full consent; Malbecco pursues her and fails to persuade her to return with him. In despair he withdraws to a cave in a wild cliff

> Where he through priuy griefe, and horrour vaine,
> Is woxen so deform'd, that he has quight
> Forgot he was a man, and *Gealosie* is hight.

(III X 60)

This is obviously a contraction of the significance of a character who is in any case a minor one. More commonly in allegory its characters acquire more meaning and power as the narrative proceeds, until they function almost like deities. In *La Divina Commedia* the process by which historical characters become representative of particular qualities or acts entails an extension of meaning. The most profound transformation and expansion is that of the character of Beatrice, who evolves from an historical character to a participant in both the pleasures and the understanding of the Divine Mind. Not only is she almost deified, but is the means by which the poet himself becomes able to contemplate the celestial vision.

> Beatrice tutta nell'etterne rote
> > fissa con li occhi stava; ed io in lei
> > le luci fissi, di là su remote.
>
> Nel suo aspetto tal dentro mi fei,
> > qual si fe' Glauco nel gustar dell'erba,
> > che 'l fe' consorte in mar delli altri Dei.
>
> Trasumanar significar per verba,
> > non si porìa; però l'essemplo basti
> > a cui esperienza grazia serba.

(*Paradiso*, I 64-72)

(Beatrice was standing with her eyes entirely fixed upon the eternal wheels: and I with my sight, remote from there

above, fixed on her. In gazing at her I became such within, as
Glaucus became in eating the herb that made him a companion
in the sea of the other gods. To express transhumanization in
words cannot be done; so let the example be enough to him
whom grace may offer the experience.)

Langland similarly modifies the figure of Piers. Initially an ordinary
fourteenth-century ploughman, though highly individuated, the
character becomes increasingly complex and potent in its associations with abstractions and theological figures. As the historical and
moral significances accumulate, Piers finally becomes equated with
Christ: *Petrus, id est Christus*. The Incarnation and the Passion are
represented by the metaphor of Christ putting on Pier's armour,
humana natura, in order to joust for the soul of man. The metaphor
would remain an inert commonplace were it not preceded by the
elaborate evolution of Piers's function in the allegorical narrative, an
evolution from a proletarian type, to counsellor and organizer, the
object of the quest, and finally to Redeemer.

Modern works of an allegorical nature, even those not overtly
theological, also display a tendency to present characters as having
divine or semi-divine natures, and as existing in an ordered hierarchy. Thus in *The Castle*, which makes no direct use of mythological, historical, or religious material, the figure of the Castellan
and the Castle itself are like sources of divine power. Barnabas, the
courier who brings messages to K., has the quality of an angelic
emissary.

> He was clothed nearly all in white, not in silk ... but the
> material he was wearing had the softness and dignity of silk.
> His face was clear and frank, his eyes larger than ordinary.
> His smile was unusually joyous; ... 'My name is Barnabas'
> said he, 'I am a messenger'. His lips were strong and yet gentle
> as he spoke.
>
> (*The Castle*, p.27)

Baron Frankenstein suffers the torments not only of creator as
artist, but of creator as God. Whereas Prometheus was punished by
the Gods, Frankenstein has suffering inflicted on him by the being
he has created. The monster is a kind of secularized Adam.

The strong links between medieval Romance and a legacy of
more primitive beliefs make it a good example of something

occurring at the mid-point between myth and allegory. The narratives show a mixture of pagan and Celtic material with Christianized legends which makes it difficult to distinguish myth from allegory or straight narrative. As a result, characters are persons, personifications, and deities. In the *Queste del Saint Graal*, the disinherited maiden who appears to Perceval on the rock, and lures him into her round tent, is only very briefly ambiguous. She is the Enemy, the master of Hell, rightly disinherited by God for pride and ambition. The round tent is the world, in which Perceval cannot remain sinless as he might in ascetic contemplation upon the rock.

Empson observed that:

... allegory itself, a comparatively late classical invention, is always liable to return to the deification from which it came

and added something that is very relevant to *Piers Plowman* with its metaphors (and its morality) so often based on rural, working-class life:

... the more you avoid this by taking a humble example of the quality as its type the more you deify the figure of pastoral.

(*Some Versions of Pastoral*, p.63)

This 'return to deification' will suggest to some readers that allegory, though more conscious, though more a vehicle for the moral and cosmic perspective of individual writers, still serves to perpetuate other kinds of 'myth'. Christian cosmology, or chivalry, or courtly eroticism as a paradigmatic social and moral experience, could be seen as the 'myths' of various societies. This is, however, to shift the definition of myth. The subject matter used by Dante, Spenser, or de Lorris is indeed often conventional, drawn from commonly shared beliefs and experiences. But the narrative in which this subject matter is contained is known to be fictional (whatever the truth of its implicit meanings), and is constantly under the control of a particular author and not of a society as a whole. Myth, often originating in the oral stage of the development of a culture, is subjected to collective pressure in ways that allegory is not.

Despite similarities in the *modus operandi* of myth and allegory, and their comparable objectives, allegory in general uses myth as only one of the means by which extra force and complexity can be given to the allegorical action and its significance. There are examples of this in two of the passages discussed in the previous section. Paridell abducts Hellenore immediately after the history of the Trojan war has been told in the preceding Canto: Paridell is thus shown as not only the lineal descendant of Paris, but as a comparable type. Dante's reference to Glaucus expresses in simile the idea of translation to a divine state – Glaucus became immortal because he ate a herb that had been sown in the Golden Age by Cronos. The materials of myth are in a sense like this unwitting gift of the god of Time; they are means by which allegorists can confer trans-temporal value on the events they describe.

Earlier allegories assert that the world is capable of being understood, that all phenomena can be seen as part of a system or order, and that this order can be revealed through analytic narrative, as in myth. Coherence and order are not easily perceived but require an elaborate process of breaking down and re-unification to become perceptible. In this process it is the reader's willingness to engage in interpretation that is crucial, and the ultimate validity of that interpretation that determines how any detail is read. Thus when authors believe that interpretation cannot lead to the discovery of real meaning the characteristics of allegory (digression, fragmentation, historical or mythological allusion) all work to frustrate the perception of order and coherence.

3   *The legible image: allegory and the visual*

One of the most important means by which interpretation is assisted and directed in allegory is its visual element. Narrative provides a basis of metaphor which expresses the ultimate purpose of the allegory and defines the limits of possible meaning: the energy of its forward movement enables the author to express process, the kinetic interrelationship between the various elements, abstractions, and powers in an imaginative system. But while both the energy and the coherence of the work derive from narrative, it is often through visual detail and imagery that the clarity of particular parts of the system and their connection with the whole is established. Details of a character's appearance, of a landscape, of architecture, help us to interpret their essential nature and to fix them in our memory, while visual similarities and connections build up a pattern of thematic association. When used unsubtly the visual can be merely mnemonic, a vehicle for dry schematization, but in the hands of a writer like Dante or Spenser it can add both intricacy and depth to the work.

Many paintings and sculptures share some of allegory's essential qualities. For example, medieval religious painting and sculpture disregard naturalistic spatio-temporal considerations in showing disproportionately large divine characters dominating a hierarchy of celestial and terrestrial beings. Historical time is telescoped by placing saints and martyrs of later centuries in attendance at the Nativity or Crucifixion; carrying their attributes they represent particular virtues and (in later medieval painting) act as sponsors to the donors who commissioned the work. These, as ordinary mortals, are often miniscule in relation to the divine beings whose acts they observe.

Even paintings and sculptures in which the 'realistic' surface is not comparably distorted or disrupted can exhibit a similar subordination of form to statement. And although such terminology sounds all too much like the echo of some tired 'form and content, debate, it has to be acknowledged that the significance – usually a significance entailing abstractions – which the artist intends the visual surface to communicate to us plays a very important part in our criticism of certain works of art. A painting like Holman Hunt's *The Awakening Conscience* cannot be seen simply in terms of a man and a woman playing the piano, as we might look at a Vermeer with comparable subject-matter. The dramatic situation and its relation to the title have to be interpreted first: the woman has suddenly been reminded of her (presumably parental) home by the tune she plays with her lover, and this has precipitated a horrified awareness of the 'immorality' of her life. From this dramatic information we are, presumably, meant to extrapolate a general statement about the assumed superiority of conventional home life over sexual irregularity. Similarly Roubiliac's monument for Lady Elizabeth Nightingale in Westminster Abbey is more than a man and a woman in pseudo-classical dress attacked by a skeleton wielding a spear. It is also something more than 'the beautiful figure of Lord Nightingale endeavouring to shield his lovely wife from death', which is how John Wesley described it: like all works in the tradition of tomb sculpture it demands that the observer makes a generalized response to the concepts of death, mortality, and human ineffectuality in the face of them.

Considerations of meaning are, it is true, not the same as considerations of value: Holman Hunt's and Roubiliac's works both appear in some degree sentimental and even over-stated. (This may of course be related to the fact that they are also both the product of centuries in which critics were openly hostile to allegory – if commonly sanctioned conventions for conveying abstract statement are unavailable, any artist is likely to use his metaphors rather uneasily.) The evaluation of such works cannot however be entirely independent of considerations of meaning, and it is noticeable that their titles, the *verbal* labels, often carry unusual weight. Iconography, even if not in the strictest sense of that word, is here a necessary adjunct to criticism. What is important for this discussion is that certain paintings and sculptures, irrespective of their particular quality, operate in ways comparable to an allegorical text. It is art which has to be read, demanding an energetic response of the observer, and the capacity to move from the particular to the general.

The paintings of Poussin also require a particular process of interpretation, a requirement to which the titles draw attention: characters are defined by visual symbols, and their relationship to one another, both in terms of composition and significance, is determined by certain preconceived abstractions. Bronzino's *Allegory* ('Venus, Cupid, Folly and Time') in the National Gallery makes comparable demands. From the lascivious central group of Venus and Cupid the eye passes to the subsidiary figures of Despair tearing her hair, and Fraud (Hypocrisy?) with her clawed feet and reversed left and right hands holding a honeycomb and a venomous insect. The entire group, which becomes increasingly sinister as each significant detail emerges from the shadows, is unveiled by Time and Truth. Not a single part of the painting can be ignored; the observer is forced to form a set of associations and to establish a hierarchy of values as he sees the interaction of the characters. In the didactic presentation of abstractions literary allegory has of course one advantage over painting: it can suggest without needing to give specific form. But it is in part the tendency in visual images to be specific and particular that makes them valuable in allegories. Allegorists constantly make use of visual detail to make the literal level of their narrative more explicit and imaginable, and to reinforce the significance of events by association.

Visual images have always functioned as aids to memory and

understanding, and in allegory striking detail and extended visual description have almost always some mnemonic function. In *The Art of Memory* (1966) Frances Yates has discussed the elaborate schemata by which classical rhetoricians suggested that images connected with particular concepts could be 'placed' in position in an imaginary building to enable a speaker to remember the content and order of a speech. This systematic visual basis for the memory had a long and curious history, not only as a practical 'applied science', but also (for men like Giulio Camillo and Ramon Lull) as a discipline with strong religious emphasis. For Giordano Bruno it was an occult art which revealed astral influences and was instrumental in teaching an Hermetic wisdom deriving from Egyptian, Greek, and Hebrew magic. The method of remembering was less important than what was remembered, and though for Bruno as for the rhetoricians this trained memory was a source of power, he saw it as offering as well a different kind of power, a magical one, to the initiate.

> Through the magic of his archetypal memory images he sees
> the groupings of nature as bound together with magical and
> associative links.   (Yates, pp.247-8)

In concluding her discussion of this apparently 'marginal subject', Dr Yates observes that:

> The history of the organisation of memory touches at vital
> points on the history of religion and ethics, of philosophy and
> psychology, of art and literature, of scientific method. The
> artificial memory as a part of rhetoric belongs into the rhetoric
> tradition; memory as a power of the soul belongs with theology.
> (*ibid.*, p.374)

The visual mnemonics of allegory similarly share a place with rhetoric, and with theology and ideology in general; the rhetorician's need for clarity produces more static images, while the needs of the theologian, the moralist, the 'peerless poet' produce an altogether more complex use of the visual in which sight becomes one of the agents by which the moral world of the allegory can be illuminated and illuminating. Ymagynatyf, that key figure in *Piers Plowman* who enables the Dreamer to reconcile experience of life with scholarly learning, is not a personification of the

Imagination in either of the senses given it by Coleridge in *Bio-graphia Literaria*. He is rather more like Fancy : 'a mode of Memory emancipated from the order of time and space'. He has been the constant companion of the Dreamer unceasingly recording and ordering events and contemplating their significance so that he may offer reminders of them to the hero. The Dreamer is precipitated into a meeting with Ymagynatyf after he has been shown by Nature the sights that teach him to see again, and restore his sense of wonder. The moral eye is restored by the natural eye. In allegory, visual images assist the reader to form a codified set of associations which are memorable and interpreted with the aid of the memory; they also intensify the moral or historical associations of given objects, persons, or events.

A renaissance scholar and commentator, Giovanni Battista Porta, makes an interesting comment on the *Aeneid* which suggests the way in which pictorial material may work in allegories, especially earlier ones. He says that the imagination draws pictures in the memory as if with a pencil, and suggests that the images decorating the temple of Juno which Dido is building, and amongst which Aeneas sees a complete and ordered record of the Trojan war, are a kind of memory system enabling Dido to remember her ancestors and their deeds together with other historical material (Yates, *The Art of Memory*, p.203). Presumably the gold plate at the banquet of welcome for the Trojans engraved 'with the heroic deeds of [the Carthaginians'] ancestors, in a long succession of historic events throughout all the generations since their nation's birth', serves a similar function. A renaissance commentator thus allegorizes the function of passages in the *Aeneid* that could be seen as merely descriptive.

The emphasis placed during the medieval period on the allegorical interpretation of sacred and literary works, and on the ordered significance of the images of ecclesiastical art, has already been discussed; scholars such as Gilson, Mâle, Panofsky, and Katzen-ellenbogen, have drawn attention to these characteristics of medieval art and to their didactic and intellectual basis. Giovanni Battista Porta wrote with critical presuppositions that were as much inherited from the medieval period as they were formed by new and 'Humanist' theories, and awareness of such presuppositions and of their longevity should suggest that it is mistaken to regard the visual element in allegory as Hazlitt regarded it in *The Faerie*

Queene. In *Lectures on the English Poets*, he says that Spenser

> becomes picturesque from his intense love of beauty; as where
> he compares Prince Arthur's crest to the appearance of the
> almond tree:
>
>> On top of greene *Selinis* all alone,
>> With blossomes braue bedecked daintily;
>> Whose tender locks do tremble euery one
> At euery little breath, that vnder heauen is blowne.
>
> [1 vii 32]
>
> The love of beauty, however, and not of truth, is the moving
> principle of his mind; and he is guided in his fantastic
> delineations by no rule but the impulse of an inexhaustible
> imagination. (Alpers, p.132)

The visual surface of the allegory and the action itself are here
emasculated of any kind of metaphysical significance, which is
strange when we consider that Hazlitt says in the same place of
Spenser that 'His ideas, indeed, seem more distinct than his perceptions. He is the painter of abstractions, and describes them with
dazzling minuteness'. Hazlitt goes on to condemn the idle fears of
those who claim that they cannot understand the poem 'on account
of the allegory'.

> If they do not meddle with the allegory, the allegory will not
> meddle with them. Without minding it at all, the whole is as
> plain as a pike-staff. It might as well be pretended that, we
> cannot see Poussin's pictures for the allegory, as that the
> allegory prevents us from understanding Spenser.
>
> (*ibid.*, p.134)

'Meddle' and 'without minding' are disabling enough indications
of the misunderstandings in Hazlitt's criticism, even without the
references to Poussin – whose work includes numerous examples of
paintings that we really *cannot* 'see' until the intended allegorical
meanings have been ascertained. The *Apollo and Daphne* and the
Acis and Galatea in the Louvre or the *Seven Sacraments* in Edin-
burgh are certainly not 'plain as a pike-staff' and no more is *The
Faerie Queene*. As with the action of allegory, its literal level, the
meanings of visual detail require constant interpretation.

The kind of visual image which requires least cross reference to the rest of the allegory is often simply mnemonic. Description, whether of appearance or attributes, serves, in Sidney's words, to 'strike, pierce, [and] possess the sight of the soul'. It yields to 'the mind an image of that whereof the philosopher bestoweth but a wordish description'. It is in medieval allegories that extensive use of this kind of visual presentation is found: static, elaborately detailed and with an immense richness of symbolic attributes. This derives partly from the medieval taste for large formal set-pieces, but more from the influence of medieval rhetoric, rhetoric in the sense of the rhetorical prescriptions found in the manuals of Geoffrey de Vinsauf or Matthew de Vendôme, rather than in the psychological sense given the term by modern critics such as Kenneth Burke. In the *Ars Versificatoria* of Matthew de Vendôme (written before 1175), two of the four books are devoted to embellishment and amplification; the first book to descriptions and the proper use of attributes, and the third to rhetorical ornament, tropes, and the embellishment of the matter of poetry. In Geoffrey de Vinsauf's *Nova Poetria*, *effictio*, the enumeration of details of external appearance, is closely linked to *notatio*, which is concerned with the description of character: the visual is thus assumed to be interdependent with other means of presenting character. (The text of both these manuals is in Faral, *Les Arts poétiques du XIIe et du XIIIe siècle*.) This emphasis on decoration and significant visual detail in literary theory offers an analogy to the belief in the social and moral significance of externals (like dress and armour) noted by historians of the period.

Both the strength and the deficiencies of this highly rhetorical use of the visual can be seen in the allegories of the late twelfth-century writer, Alain de Lille. In the *Anticlaudianus* Nature appears to the poet wearing a twelve-starred crown, with the twelve jewels miraculously turning and changing to represent the signs of the Zodiac, a robe ornamented with pictures of terrestrial life, all the animals and birds, a mantle decorated with images of the ocean's inhabitants, and a shift and slippers embroidered with herbs, fruit and trees. The portrait has both charm and elegance in its minutiae and in the encyclopaedic inclusiveness. Unfortunately, the poet over-emphasizes the visual nature of what he describes, its existence as a collection of actual images 'such as commonly painted' or 'like sculptures', contained within the one large-scale portrait of Nature. This emphasis is irreconcilable with his interest (typical of an allegorist) in suggestive associations, encyclopaedism, and the moral and metaphysical implications of every detail. He tries to give an ordered and comprehensible picture of Nature as a cosmic force revealed in all the created world, but order and comprehensibility break down when on the one hand he constantly reminds the reader that this is literally a visual 'image', and on the other hand cannot resist any opportunity to connect sense experience with an altogether more speculative mode of imagining what Nature might be like. Alain's ideas do indeed 'seem more distinct than his perceptions', despite his relentless insistence on the actuality of the latter.

Nature's mantle carries pictures of fish – a perfectly acceptable allusion to one part of the creation. But words like *sculpturae* and *picturae* hammer home the point that these are intended to be seen as *actual* objects, as artefacts, rather than as imaginatively suggestive details. The not altogether happy influence of prescriptive rhetoric on Alain de Lille's allegory is betrayed by the phrase 'pictured tropes' (*tropo picturae*). The literary trope can make use of our visual imagination, but it cannot convey both the photographic exactness of a picture, *and* the dynamic suggestiveness of metaphor. Allegory, which extends metaphor into a complex narrative, needs the visual as a basis for dramatic action, but description of figures or objects should help to differentiate concepts, not contain them.

Alain derives the action of the *De Planctu Naturae* from the complaint, an essentially undynamic form. His grasp of dramatic action is simply not strong enough to offset the great set-pieces such as the portrait of Nature, or the *descriptio loci* of the House of Fortune in Volume VII viii, of the *Anticlaudianus*. He also has a passion for symbolic attributes and associations. Grammar, the first of the seven liberal arts in the *Anticlaudianus*, carries a scalpel, Dialectic flowers and a scorpion. These are both conventional attributes in a tradition deriving from Martianus Capella's *Marriage of Mercury and Philology*. The scalpel is a dentist's instrument for polishing and cutting the teeth; it indicates the basis of Grammar in the spoken word, as well as symbolizing its curative and 'pruning' function in language. Flowers and a scorpion show the combination in Dialectic of the brilliance of perfect syllogism with the sting and tortuousness of sophistry. Neither of these attributes can be interpreted without recourse to knowledge external to the text, nor have they any obvious association with the nature of Grammar or Dialectic as revealed in an allegorical action. If the allegorist portrays characters holding flowers, or a scalpel, or a scorpion, readers may remember the conventional significance of such visual details and be able to interpret them. But it is still an emblematic, static method, and does not necessarily contribute to the analysis of the allegorical action in its entirety. Such emblems and 'pictured tropes' work through adjectives and nouns, not verbs, and it is ultimately upon verbs that the substance of allegory relies.

Langland, who is somewhat un-medieval in his lack of emphasis on visual detail, is unexpectedly vivid in the portraits of the Seven Deadly Sins in Book v of *Piers Plowman*. The reason that they are so successful in allegorical terms is that the purely visual is held in balance with the dramatic by his device of making the Sins reveal their own character in confession, and sometimes act out what they are confessing.

And þanne cam coueytise . can I hym nouȝte descryue,
So hungriliche and holwe . sire Heruy hym loked.
He was bitelbrowed . and baberlipped also,
With two blered eyghen . as a blynde hagge;
And as a letheren purs . lolled his chekes,
Wel sydder þan his chyn . þei chiueled for elde;
And as a bondman of his bacoun . his berde was bidraueled.
With an hode on his hed . a lousi hatte aboue,
And in a tauny tabarde . of twelue wynter age,
Al totorne and baudy . and ful of lys crepynge;
But if þat a lous couthe . haue lopen þe bettre,
She sholde nouȝte haue walked on þat welche . so was it
                                                    thredebare.
                                    (*Piers Plowman*, v 188-99)

(And then came Covetousness; I can't describe him, so hungry and hollow that Sir Hervy looked. He was beetle-browed and flabby-lipped too, with two gummy eyes like an old blind hag; and his cheeks sagged like a leather purse down below his chin, and trembled with age; his beard was all besmeared, like a serf's with his bacon fat. He had a hood on his head and a lousy hat on top, and wore a brownish smock twelve years old, and all torn and filthy and full of crawling lice. But even a louse, if it could have found its way to jump somewhere better, wouldn't have walked on that it was so threadbare.)

This third-person description is essentially a preface to Covetous-ness's first-person autobiographical confession.

The allegorist who ignores the action in a series of descriptions discards an essential part of allegory. Langland is working in the tradition of sermons (an aspect of *Piers Plowman* discussed by G. R. Owst in *Literature and Pulpit in Medieval England*), and this in part explains his ability to organize and contain description. A preacher, for whom didactic clarity was all important, could certainly make good use of vivid 'pictures' – they functioned as a well-chosen analogy may for a talented political speaker. For an audience that was in large part un-lettered, visual images would have had considerable value, and these had additional authority if their symbols or attributes had well-known Biblical or even classical antecedents. But the fable or parable, crude forms of allegory, are also a basic device for the sermon, and in these action is all important. Langland knew, as a good contemporary preacher must have done, how to moderate his allegory between image and action. Thus Lady Mede is both an overdressed rich woman and the Scarlet Woman of the Apocalypse:

> ... a womman . wortheli yclothed,
> Purfiled with pelure . þe finest upon erthe,
> Y-crounede with a corone . þe kyng hath non better.
> Fetislich her fyngres . were fretted with golde wyre.
> And þere-on red rubyes . as red as any glede,
> And diamantz of derrest pris . and double manere safferes,
> Orientales and ewages . enuenymes to destroye.
> Hire robe was ful riche . of red scarlet engreyned,
> With ribanes of red golde . and of riche stones;
>
> (*Piers Plowman*, II 8-16)

(a woman, finely dressed, adorned with furs, the finest on earth, and crowned with a crown – the king has no better. Her fingers were elaborately clasped with gold rings, set with red rubies as red as a red-hot coal, and the most expensive diamonds, and double-sized sapphires, and amethysts and beryls able to destroy poisons. Her robe was rich and costly, dyed scarlet red, with ribbons and ornaments of red gold and precious stones.)

The description contains suggestions of the usurpation of true temporal power, and of the red hot fires of Hell, but these suggestions are amplified when Langland goes on to show what the personification really represents (i.e. the power and perniciousness of money), in an account of her devious activities and the way she is desired, cajoled, fought for, hated, and roughly dismissed – which is surely the only adequate way to give an account of the operations of money and material reward in society.

To demonstrate the difference between 'static' visual images and those which are integrated with the substance of the allegory, two further examples from medieval literature – chosen almost at random – may be considered. In *The Castel of Love* there is an almost laboriously concrete visual image of a castle which represents the Virgin Mary (ed. Horstmann, lines 667-858). Its foundations are green, and symbolize the Virgin's constantly renewed faith, for green never loses its colour, and is the sign of the renewal of life in nature. The middle section of the castle is blue, standing for her hope, and the topmost parts, red 'as though burning', show her love. The four forts are her possession of the four cardinal virtues, the inmost bailey her virginity, the middle one her chastity, and the outermost her marriage; the seven barbicans are the seven virtues, and the wells in the centre of the castle the springs of the Virgin's grace, which 'soccoureth all the world yet'. The description of the castle is a mechanical device to demonstrate the attributes of the Virgin, and serves to fix the attention of the reader and assist memory. It does not show the Virgin's moral perfection in any organic way, or interrelate with the rest of the poem. By contrast, the descriptions of Youth, Maturity and Old Age in the *Parlement of the Thre Ages* (ed. Offord) interact throughout with the substance of their philosophies of life as expressed in their debate. Youth is extravagantly and showily dressed, his manner has the nonchalant ease of the courtier, and his bearing is military. His appearance thus demonstrates his delight in immediate pleasure : nothing would induce him to sell his jewels for investments as Middle Age advises, since he knows that the reward for scrimping and saving is ultimately to see someone else come 'and spend what you have long spared'. He prefers to court his 'perfection among paramours, his lady with sweet breasts', or to stand with 'a fierce sharpened sword boldly in his hand'. John Speirs (1950) has suggested that the author of the *Parlement* may have had in mind the roles of actors in a pageant and certainly the poem reveals an ability to make the visual instrumental in a dramatic presentation of the life styles and ideas for which each of the three characters stand.

The kind of visual description that is found in an overblown form in Alain de Lille, and in a naïve one in *The Castel of Love*, is the simplest level at which image and personification interact – the visual equivalent to the simple repetitive action of the masque or progress. It is static allegory and its intricacies often do not impinge upon the action at all. This method, by which a personification announces and fulfils its characteristics through its appearance, is most effective when limited to small-scale or easily defined ideas: Gluttony, Justice, Avarice, or Grammar, rather than Hope, or Nature, or Charity. It is, of course, best suited to the presentation of human types, even if these types are given some kind of abstract or metaphysical status by being included in a theological grouping such as the Seven Deadly Sins. And in the nature of things it is much easier to give sharply visual form to Vices than to Virtues, to subsidiary categories than to major concepts. Gluttony looks what he is by being grossly fat, cramming food into his mouth, swilling drink, vomiting, and stumbling. In the descriptions of personifications such as these there is necessarily a confusion of agent and patient: Jealousy is shown as making other people jealous and also as suffering the pains of jealousy.

Visual images of this kind are frequently found in sets in allegories: the Virtues, the Vices, the Seasons, Cupid's saints, the characters on the outside of the Garden of Mirth in *Le Roman de la Rose*. Each member of the latter set represents a quality – whether accidental, such as Poverty or Old Age, or emotional, such as Envy – which disables men from becoming one of the company of true lovers. Because they are all painted on the outside of the Garden, they form a category of exclusions which are then necessarily cross-referenced. In such groups of allegorical images, it is often more important to cross-refer within the given group than to the allegorical action as a whole.

Spenser may sometimes use visual detail in a static, mnemonic way, but this method of conveying meaning through the visual and external is soon supplemented by action. For example, both Fidelia and Speranza, the 'two most goodly virgins' who greet Redcrosse

and Una in the House of Holinesse, are initially described in terms
of their attributes. Fidelia

> ... was araied all in lilly white,
> And in her right hand bore a cup of gold,
> With wine and water fild vp to the hight,
> In which a Serpent did himselfe enfold,
> That horrour made to all, that did behold;
> But she no whit did chaunge her constant mood:
> And in her other hand she fast did hold
> A booke, that was both signd and seald with blood,
> Wherein darke things were writ, hard to be vnderstood.

> Her younger sister, that *Speranza* hight,
> Was clad in blew, that her beseemed well; ...
> Vpon her arme a siluer anchor lay,
> Whereon she leaned euer....

(I X 13-14)

The images are established quickly (only a stanza for each) and are
immediately followed by dialogue between Una and Redcrosse and
the two Virtues, who then undertake his instruction and initiation.
The pictorial is only a prelude to action; Spenser places the virtues
within the conventions of Christian iconography and then sub-
sumes these conventions into the particular mode of action of *The
Faerie Queene*.

Spenser is really a lot cannier about his use of the pictorial and the
'picturesque' than Hazlitt could possibly have understood. Far from
being 'guided ... by no rule but the impulse of an inexhaustable
imagination', the 'fantastic delineations' of *The Faerie Queene* reveal
a capacity to create both visual images as schematic as those of the
De Planctu Naturae and *The Castel of Love* (for example, the House
of Alma in Book II, Canto ix), and also others which are intricately
connected with the ideological purpose and imaginative texture of
the poem. By isolating the former kind by presenting them as
paintings, or tapestries, or as characters in a masque (i.e., as an
internally cross-referenced group), he reveals his awareness of the
different quality and function of mnemonic images, and makes it
easier for the reader to interpret them in the right way. Alter-
natively, he sometimes makes the visually schematic an element in
the landscape or setting in which an important event occurs – the

Garden of Adonis, the House of Alma, Acrasia's Bower of Bliss, Mount Acidale.

Spenser has a characteristic talent for presenting a visual picture and then modifying it through a simile or metaphor so that the limitations of the visual dimension are broken by secondary suggestions, often dependent on verbs. For example, the captain of the enemy host assailing the House of Alma is described very precisely (II xi 20-2) but he is 'of such subtle substance and vnsound,/That like a ghost he seem'd, whose graue-clothes were vnbound.' Belphoebe's legs are 'Like two faire marble pillours .../Which doe the temple of the Gods support,/Whom all the people decke with girlands greene,/And honour in their festiuall resort' (II iii 28). The visual comparison is extended into associations of holiness and festivity.

It is necessary that description in allegory should be extended dramatically because of the basis of the form in metaphysical systems; the most important aspects of such systems are necessarily shown in the interaction of different elements. Emphasis on significant detail of a character's appearance in order to typify some particular quality is not of course the prerogative of allegory, but is to be found in other forms of literature. Many novels (those of Dickens would be an obvious example) and plays in which characterization is overtly based on types, provide examples of the visual endowed with metaphysical and abstract significance. It is a common mental habit to equate the external with the internal, or with some abstract meaning. (Gombrich discusses this 'physiognomic' reading of works of art or images in *Meditations on a Hobby Horse*.) There are important differences between this sporadic use of the visual to make important secondary meanings clear, and the much more extended use of it in allegorical writing. First, all the figures in allegory tend in some degree to be presented in this way, i.e. almost any visual detail is 'significant'; second, the expectations of metaphysical, ideological, and abstract significances which are aroused by allegory mean that readers are quite properly ready to see in visual details a significance that might pass unnoticed in more mimetic literature.

The heavily charged nature of the visual surface in allegory is often most apparent in the descriptions of setting or landscape rather than of characters. A location is necessarily more inert than a person; description of it cannot therefore be 'extended dramatically'. Despite this, the dramatic acts which happen in a given location can interact with the description of it, and our interpretation of the allegorical meaning of those acts can be assisted by visual details in the description of the setting. The setting in which an allegorical action occurs is always activated by the significance of the narrative. At its most crudely schematic this is to be found in Piers the Ploughman's directions to the pilgrims who are searching for Truth:

> turn down by the stream *Be-gentle-in-speech*, till you come to a ford, *Honour-thy-father-and-mother*. There you must wade into the water and wash yourselves thoroughly, then you'll step more lightly for the rest of your life. ... you will come to a hill, *Bear-no-false-witness*. Turn right away from it, for it is thickly wooded with bribes, and bristling with florins.
>
> (trans. Goodridge, pp.116-17)

The passage in its entirety is a kind of Ordnance Survey of the Decalogue. The weight of prescription here destroys the notional view of an actual landscape as the emblematic characterization of the Virgin does the actual image of the castle in *The Castel of Love*. A more intelligent version of this is to be found in the geography of *The Pilgrim's Progress*: both Langland and Bunyan are probably influenced by the kind of devices used mnemonically by preachers. A faint echo of the same device occurs in the names of places in the Romances – the Siege Perilous, Joyous Gard, and so on.

An allegory may sometimes lack a specific visual setting, particularly if the action presented is highly abstract, but when there is a setting it is never inert. The wilds and pastures of *The Faerie Queene* are as much an example of this as the set-pieces like the Garden of Adonis. In *La Divina Commedia*, the landscapes through which Virgil and Dante pass are always presented in emphatically explanatory, and even realistic, ways. But the astrological and geographical 'exactness' is in itself an instrument by which the connections between the material world of the senses (in which the reader lives) and the imagined world beyond space and time are underlined. Dante asks his guide the source of the red river, Phlegethon, in *Inferno*, XIV. Virgil describes the 'ancient figure' standing on Mount Ida in Crete: its head is gold, its arms and torso silver, then brass to the groin, and its legs and feet are iron, save only the right foot which is clay, and which bears almost the full weight of the figure. The image is fractured right through

> d'una fessura che lagrime goccia,
> le quali, accolte, foran quella grotta.
> Lor corso in questa valle si diroccia :
> fanno Acheronte, Stige e Flegetonta;
>> (*Inferno*, XIV 113-16)

(with a fissure that drops tears, which, gathered together, bore through that cave. Their course descends from rock to rock into this valley : they form Acheron, Styx, and Phlegethon.)

This image, partly derived from Daniel's vision in Daniel, ii 31-5, and partly from Ovid's description of the Four Ages in *Metamorphoses*, I, is in itself a complex visual symbolization of the history of mankind and of the tension between secular and ecclesiastical power (the clay foot) on which mankind leans most heavily. Dante's enquiries are not directed to the meanings of the image, however, but towards apparent geographical improbability; why, if the water dropping from the fissures falls straight down through the earth into this valley, have they only just caught sight of it? Virgil reminds him that their journey has been taking a leftwards circular descent ('Tu sai che il loco è tondo') and that they have not yet turned through the full circle. This is an extremely sophisticated use of visual description : for a start it is not something which they actually see, but the source elsewhere of something that they actually see which Virgil describes, as any poet might. Yet because the image is so detailed, and because the emphasis is on its realistically and materially curious aspect, it *seems* to be there, and gives us a sense of a strange (and exciting) dislocation of space and time. It is a reminder that everything Dante sees in Hell has its source in the past (the Four Ages of the world), and in earthly experience. Each description of a new landscape that opens up similarly gives the effect of co-existing multiple layers of time and space. The allusions and comparisons to places in Italy do not make us feel that the landscape of the *Commedia* is *as* real as the Italian one, but that it is more real.

The concern for plausibility, geographical, scientific, and astronomical, is very much a Dantesque feature of allegorical topography. Generally, it is the kind of landscape, what it evokes, that is important. No commentator could supply plans, charts, and maps to Langland or Bunyan or Spenser as they have done for Dante. In *Gulliver's Travels* Swift predictably plays with the notion of exactitude: though some times and dates, and longitudes and latitudes, are given, Gulliver complains in the letter to Cousin Sympson that

> your printer hath been so careless as to confound the times, and mistake the dates of my several voyages and returns. . . .

In Sympson's letter, 'The Publisher to the Reader', it is 'admitted' that he has

> made bold to strike out innumerable passages relating to the winds and tides, as well as to the variations and bearings in the several voyages. . . .

By explaining the absence of realistic precision in realistic terms, the illusion of the actuality of Gulliver's voyages is strengthened, while the fictitiousness is preserved. Of course, Dante wished the illusion of his journey to be as acceptable to rationality as possible because he wished us to consider his view of the metaphysical structures, of which the journey is an external form, as truth. Swift, whose aims are predominantly satirical, is concerned that we should accept the truth of the criticisms of human nature, of human beings' inflated and over-refined view of themselves, which are inherent in Gulliver's experience, rather than any 'truth' about the cosmos.

For Spenser, the location of certain of his heroes' centrally important actions carries very great weight. Sir Guyon, the knight of Temperance, is a

> . . . Pilot well expert in perilous waue,
> That to a stedfast starre his course hath bent, . . .
> Vpon his card and compas firmes his eye,
> The maisters of his long experiment,
> And to them does the steddy helme apply. . . .
>
> (II vii I)

He is equipped to find his way about the landscape of allegory; as the representative of that Virtue that enables us to shun extremes he is his own compass, he 'can measure out a theme' of virtuous

behaviour. When he descends with Mammon into the earth he is
led into a cave:

> Therein an hundred raunges weren pight,
> And hundred fornaces all burning bright;
> By euery fornace many feends did bide,
> Deformed creatures, horrible in sight,
> And euery feend his busie paines applide,
> To melt the golden metall, ready to be tride.
>
> One with great bellowes gathered filling aire,
> And with forst wind the fewell did inflame;
> Another did the dying bronds repaire
> With yron toungs, and sprinckled oft the same
> With liquid waues, fiers *Vulcans* rage to tame,
> Who maistring them, renewd his former heat;
> (II vii 35-6)

This for the Money God is the 'fountaine of the worldes good',
while for Guyon it is quite the opposite: but the description of
the cave of the furnaces is not just a description of a great gold
factory – it is also a reminder of the burning effect of extreme
passion. Guyon's descent into the Cave of Mammon is immediately
preceded by an account of Pyrochles (who stands for Wrath),
throwing himself into a lake to assuage the hot fire that Furor has
'Kindled through his infernall brond of spight'. Atin, Pyrochles'
squire, the same that has *Burnt I doe burne* on his shield, sees
him plunging around in the water, and demands the matter

> I burne, I burne, I burne, then loud he cryde,
> O how I burne with implacable fire,
> Yet nought can quench mine inly flaming syde,
> Nor sea of licour cold, nor lake of mire,
> Nothing but death can doe me to respire.
> (II vi 44)

The unquenchable fires of Mammon are significantly associated
with the fires of rage. When Guyon arrives at Acrasia's Bower of
Blisse, the description also conveys a sense of stifling heat. The
enchantress is laid on a bed of roses 'As faint through heat, or dight
to pleasant sin', her breast glistens with sweat from her 'late sweet
toyle', and her eyes

Moystend their fierie beames, with which she thrild
Fraile harts, yet quenched not. ...

(II xii 78)

The visual details of Mammon's and Acrasia's dwellings, with their emphasis on heat, offer a deliberate opposition to the theme of water as a source of grace which runs through the whole book. This latter theme has been discussed by Alastair Fowler (1960), who observes that there are two kinds of water in the book: the first is both the fountain of repentance and the baptismal bath of regeneration; the second the 'liquid ioyes' of profane, sensual love. 'Contrasted images of water are, indeed, the Book's leitmotiv.' The visual details which suggest fire and heat in the accounts of the Cave of Mammon, the torment of Pyrochles, and Acrasia's Bower are in contrast to the first set of symbolic meanings for water. The description of the Captain of the hosts of the Senses which assault the House of Alma (quoted in part above) also includes the detail that he looked 'pale and wan as ashes' – the residue of consuming fire.

When the external surface of description is thus intimately connected with the ideological and metaphysical patterns of the narrative, the image does indeed serve to show us 'the groupings of nature as bound together with magical and associative links'. The settings of The Faerie Queene are always full of associations revealing the particular power of the soul that is being demonstrated at the time; these settings are rich in images with classical (and of course in Book II, theological) connections. If nothing else, landscape is in sympathy with the mood and emotion of the action performed in it.

Architectural settings in allegory similarly display the 'pathetic fallacy' at work (except that it is less fallacious, since architecture is made, an artefact, and can therefore with more probability and propriety reflect the moods, intentions, and priorities of human beings). In Mervyn Peake's trilogy of fantastic narratives, Titus Groan, Gormenghast and Titus Alone, architecture is both microcosm and macrocosm; there is nothing beyond the fabricated environment. The castle of Gormenghast is an architectural image which telescopes an entire vision of the world, a monstrous inflation of a particular, private, Gothick world. The castle, 'the Stones' as it is called, is both a human mind (particularly Titus's mind because the castle is the symbol of his inheritance), and also the accretion of several human minds. It is so vast that none of its inhabitants knows it perfectly or even adequately. For Fuschia, Titus's elder sister, for Flay, the devoted butler, and for Titus and the other characters, the Stones have an entirely different architecture. It only comes to have a common appearance and topography during the great Flood (which is an agent from outside), when the inhabitants are also united by the hunt for the murderous and treacherous enemy within the castle, Steerpike. The immense, rambling, endless architecture of Gormenghast is in decay, and its decay is the decay of systems outside the allegorical world of the book, as well as inside it. Because it is decayed, much of it is abandoned, and this abandonment allows the individuals within it to find out and guard special, secret, private worlds which meet their needs in a way the common life of the castle cannot. Architecture thus functions pathetically for individuals, but is also a literary and metaphysical image denoting the impossibility of any single macrocosmic pattern of conceptual topography.

Because architecture is man-made and artificial, it enables Peake to present states of mind with minute regard to texture and appearance as correlatives: stone, rotten wood, dust, shining acres of roof, brilliant and flaking paint, private cubby holes, vast halls. It is also a supreme setting for 'Gothick' consciousness in that morbidity, decay, and desolation are unredeemed by any natural cyclic process. The most sympathetic characters all have some ability to exist in or show interest in a world outside the castle, a more natural world: both Titus and Flay survive an existence outside the castle. By contrast, Barquentine, who is Lord of the Library and Keeper of the Groan Lore, is dry corruption in both person and intellect: he is simply concerned with the preservation of ancient ritual, and the instant in which he leaves the castle is also the instant of his death. The vast scale of the architecture makes overt the idea of a tradition, an accumulation of immemorial man-directed action, that is so unwieldy that even those who live most directly under its rule cannot know its meaning or extent. The Groan Lore, the rituals of Gormenghast, are imprisoning: 'Centuries of experience had seen to it that there should be no gap in the steady, intricate stream of immemorial behaviour' (*Titus Groan*, p.333).

The scale of the visual setting also gives the action a heroic dimension, both the inverted heroism of Steerpike's burning of the Library (a would-be revolutionary act that does not have precisely the desired effect), and the true heroic of Titus's final battle with Steerpike. The scale is suggested not only by the long and fantastic descriptions, but also by passages like the following. The Countess summons her constant companions, the white cats:

> From a hundred dim recesses, from favourite ledges, from
> shelves and draught-proof corners, from among the
> tattered entrails of old sofas, from the scarred plush of chairs,
> from under clock-stands, from immemorial sun-traps, and
> from nests of claw-torn paper – from the inside of lost
> hats, from among rafters, from rusty casques, and from
> drawers half-open, the cats poured forth, converged,
> foamed, and with a rapid pattering of their milk-white feet
> filled up the corridors, and a few moments later had reached
> the landing and were on their way, in the wake of their
> great mistress, down the stairway they obscured.
> (Gormenghast, p.316)

The castle has analogies with the Daedalian maze, but Gormenghast has no Minotaur at the centre, because there is no heart to the building, no focus, architectural or moral; even Steerpike, who is directly responsible for at least six deaths, is not the source of evil but only an agent. There is absolutely no morality underlying any of the deaths, either those that are Steerpike's responsibility, or those others which are gruesomely accidental.

Architecture is used as one form of significant visual level in a number of allegories. *Titus Groan* and *Gormenghast*, and even the more sketchy *Titus Alone*, are remarkable because of the sheer weight of significance that each description of the architecture, or parts of it, carries. Gormenghast castle dominates the first two books and is almost more important than the characters; if these were not also minutely and vividly described, the allegorical setting would threaten to overwhelm the action as personification overwhelms action in the *De Planctu Naturae*. The narrative of the trilogy is unlike older allegories; neither action nor setting represents a coherent view of the world. Peake offers us a richly fantastic narrative (it would be very difficult to call it a novel) with obvious secondary meanings, allegorical and symbolic, in all its phases. But though the setting of the narrative is *locally* allegorical, in its entirety it reveals the same kind of individualism that is to be found in Kafka's treatment of the Castle or the Courts of the Law : there is no single view of the Stones. Every corner, every corridor, has a different perspective for each character. In this respect Peake's work is like Melville's *Moby Dick*, where the sea and the blank whiteness of the whale, are *tabulae rasae* onto which each individual projects his own particular 'ungraspable phantom' : the method is allegorical, but the total effect is of allegory *à rebours* – no single meaning or place in a pattern of meaning can be claimed for any thing seen.

A castle is obviously an unavoidably aristocratic and fantastic visual setting; both *Piers Plowman* and *The Pilgrim's Progress* employ in general an altogether more democratized and commonplace setting for the action. The visual style of these works derives either from well-known Biblical, popular, or popular-classical sources, or from some matrix of common experience (as does also the tap-room in *The Castle*). In Chaucer, in Ariosto, in Tasso (whom Galileo saw as having a rigid, static, fragmentary visual style which he called 'intarsiated'), or in Spenser, the aristocratic landscape and setting is the norm. This is not merely because pastoral and Romance are usually aristocratic forms, but because most of these poets deliberately make us see these settings through an aristocratic style. An aristocratic style, after all, makes possible all kinds of refinements of hierarchy. Quite often, though – particularly in the case of Spenser – we find that the phantoms or delights that are described in terms of aristocratic or highly literary images have popular origins :

> We have long looked for the origins of *The Faerie Queene* in
> Renaissance palaces and Platonic academies, and forgotten
> that it has humbler origins of at least equal importance
> in the Lord Mayor's show, the chap-book, the bedtime story,
> the family Bible, and the village church. What lies next beneath
> the surface in Spenser's poem is the world of popular
> imagination : almost a popular mythology.
> (Lewis, *The Allegory of Love*, p.312)

The images of allegory, if they are not to be mere clutter around the neck of the meaning (or for that matter the story, to concede a point in Hazlitt's direction), must achieve something of this quality of 'a popular mythology'. They must aid the memory and the imagination to understand the significances of the action, and to perceive connections and make associations. The sort of schematic spelling-out of *The Castel of Love* or Piers's directions to the Pilgrims is really so little removed from the tract that it might as well be one. It is the relentless explicitness (as with Alain de Lille) that is the danger: it denies the possibility of reading intelligently, deprives us of the pleasure of cumulative understanding and inter-pretation, and thus makes us feel that the image as image is not worth understanding. We need to be able to use our own visual experience along with our own memories to some extent, so that what we see in the visual dimension of allegory is activated by our own perceptions. Chapman wrote of such interaction in the Sixt Sestyad of his continuation of Marlowe's *Hero and Leander*:

> as you beholde
> Sometimes within the Sunne a face of golde,
> Form'd in strong thoughts, by that traditions force,
> That saies a God sits there and guides his course.
>   (ed. Tucker Brooke, p.546)

We cannot follow Hazlitt's advice not to 'meddle' with the visual surface of allegory, its 'fantastic delineations': if we do so, we squander both one of the most important sources of meaning and significance and the proper pleasure of reading this kind of literature. Both 'strong thoughts' and 'traditions force' should be operative in our interpretation of the visual element in literary allegory, as they are equally the means by which we 'read' the allegorical meanings in a painting by Bronzino or Poussin.

3

The possibilities of allegory: freedoms and limitations

1 Freedom: timelessness, complexity, enigma

Starting from the premiss that the allegorist has persuasive or didactic designs on his readers, the previous chapters have been concerned with the means by which he can give clarity and coherence to the exposition of his ideas. By separating out various aspects of a concept or process into a multiplicity of persons or personifications, by placing related notions in sets or categories or in more or less self-contained dramatic units, by the use of visual detail and thematic and symbolic images, above all by the overall development of the allegory, he controls and directs the reader's interpretation. But to talk of 'control' and 'direction' makes it sound as if Frye's comment that 'continuous allegory prescribes the direction of commentary and thus its freedom' (*Anatomy*, p.90) were the whole truth about allegory.

All literary works impose certain limitations on our interpretative freedoms, and allegory – certainly great allegories like Spenser's or Dante's as opposed to minor, more mechanistic ones like *The Castel of Love* – is really not the rigid form it is sometimes supposed to be. Elasticity and room for manœuvre through shades of meaning are provided not only by the reader's imagination, his 'strong thoughts', his own experience of tradition, his own memory, but by the massiveness and enigma of the central concepts. Allegorists do not merely take for granted that there will be tension and interplay between the reader's consciousness and the elements in the work which operate on that consciousness – presumably a truism about all reading – but also take specific steps to suggest that their central ideas and images cannot be strait-jacketed by a single set of controls.

Rosemond Tuve, writing of the 'thoroughgoing metaphorical nature of allegory' comments that:

> Like the neighboring trope of irony, metaphor implies what
> it can not overtly state without losing the formal
> character which defines it as a figure; both figures are,
> as it were, open at one end, allowing interpretations which
> can be supported by proper evidence but not proven. An
> extreme, perhaps a peculiar, complexity is given to the
> openness in the case of allegory by the fact that we read the
> 'letter' figuratively, meanings appear which we can
> arguably claim are and were always there, though we may
> know without doubt that the writer of 'the letter'
> did not see them.
>
> (Tuve, p.220)

The mode is ironic in that images and figures are simultaneously one thing *and* another or several others, and also reveals a deliberately willed ambiguity in the recurrence of double plots and identities, transformations and metempsychosis, the fantastic, and – very importantly – by the ways in which the concept of time operates. Time and the historical sense are presented as relative, and what one might vulgarly call the 'great moments' of many allegories obviously attempt to create a sense of timelessness and a-temporality. It is also at such moments that the mythopœic aspect of allegory is most strongly felt.

When Langland describes the Harrowing of Hell, or Kafka the Castle, or Spenser the Cave of Mammon, we do not respond to those events and places as if they existed in the isolation of the single work, but as assimilating a weight of analogy. Our perceptions are compounded of the details in the present work and our memories of other similar events in other reading. The Harrowing is a single supremely dramatic moment, but also echoes non-dramatic treatments of the same subject, and incorporates a wealth of related reference and allusion.

Efte þe liȝte bad vnlouke . & Lucifer answered,
'What lorde artow?' quod lucifer . 'quis es iste?'

'*Rex glorie*'. þe liȝte sone seide,
'And lorde of myȝte & of mayne . & al manere vertues;
                                    dominus virtutum;
Dukes of þis dym place. anon vndo þis ȝates,
That cryst may come in. þe kynges sone of heuene.'
And with þat breth helle brake. with Beliales barres;
For any wye or warde. wide opene þe ȝatis.
Patriarkes & prophetes. *populus in tenebris*,
Songen seynt Iohanes songe. *ecce agnus dei*.
Lucyfer loke ne myȝte. so liȝte hym ableynte.
And þo þat owre lorde loued. in-to his liȝte he lauȝte. ...

(*Piers Plowman*, XVIII 313-324)

(Then the light commanded them to unlock and Lucifer
answered : 'What Lord art thou?' said Lucifer, 'Who
is this?'. 'The king of glory' the Light said at once, 'And lord
of might and of power and all manner of virtues; the lord
of virtues; Dukes of this dim place, undo these gates
now, that Christ may come in, the King of Heaven's Son'.
And with that breath Hell broke, with all the bars of
Belial, despite guards and warders the gates broke wide open.
Patriarchs and prophets, the people in darkness, sang
St. John's song : Behold the Lamb of God. Lucifer might not
look, the light so blinded him. And those that our Lord
loved he caught up into his light.)

The quotations from the Psalms and from Matthew and John stand
out because they are in Latin; but there is a further allusiveness in
that the 'light' which is Christ is both a weapon of cruel illumina-
tion, such as the light which blinded Saul on the Damascus road,
and also, in association with 'breath', the power of God which
carried Elijah up into heaven.

Guyon's descent into the Cave of Mammon is similarly rich in
allusions : it is a particular test confronting a single hero, but also
echoes heroic descents into a dangerous underworld – the Christian
hell, folkloric underworlds such as the Cave of the Nibelungs,
and those of classical myth such as that in the *Aeneid*. The Castle
is both the particular building K. sees and also the multitude of
castles of quest and Romance. Our memories associate and marry
the immediate particularity with its archetypes.

All the earlier allegories make extensive use of the sense of the past – not only the fruits of that past in the particular associations and meanings of a given image, but also a generalized sense of the lapse of time. In *The Faerie Queene* the reader's awareness of classical myth and the chivalric past, or in *The Pilgrim's Progress* of the biblical past, is exploited to give depth and detail to the action. In many cases such awareness is stimulated by implicit or explicit allusions to a literary past: in a poem like *The Parlement of Foules* Chaucer makes literary allusion the ground work on which the vision rests. It is not simply that the past gives authority to the meanings and values of so many allegories; rather, the sense of the past and of previous civilizations becomes a source of explanations of an imagined but relevant present. An idealized supra-temporal process, represented by the allegorical fiction, derives value from the interpenetration of several cultures or of several stages of culture. When Arthur and Guyon are in the House of Alma they experience the 'wonder of antiquitie' in reading their respective ancestries, Arthur's deriving from Brutus and Guyon's from Prometheus' first creation (*The Faerie Queene*, II x). This is one of the more overt examples of 'history' being incorporated into the allegory to give an extra dimension to the heroes and their actions. In *La Divina Commedia* the historical element is both more accurate and more pervasive – it consists of events remembered by those whom Dante meets, rather than a fictional chronicle encapsulated in discovered volumes, as are the ancestries of Arthur and Guyon. Both Spenser and Dante introduce the temporal perspective to give additional seriousness and depth to the central action and its significance. The procedure is a kind of simultaneous diachronism.

Allegory is also a mode that is cavalier with the sequential, often intentionally. Unlike the usual novel, the narrative does not even try to preserve the illusion of a sequence of acts during which a realistic lapse of time is felt. *La Divina Commedia* is unusual in emphasizing the hour-by-hour chronology of the poet's vision, as it is in the references to the relative nature of that chronology when considered in spatial terms. When Dante gazes on Beatrice at the beginning of the *Paradiso* the sun is at its zenith, but the brilliancy of noon is contrasted with the blackness of the other hemisphere.

Fatto avea di là mane e di qua sera
tal foce quasi, e tutto era là bianco
quello emisperio, e l'altra parte nera. ...
                                   (*Paradiso*, I 43-5)

(This point – i.e. the point from which the sun rises at the
equinox – had almost made morning there and evening
here, and all there in that hemisphere was brilliant,
and this other region black.)

Dante used temporal reference as he so often used visual and topo-
graphical detail, to give veracity to the vision. Even so, his 'modest
reluctance to apply mundane categories to the trans-temporal'
(which A. D. Nuttall comments on) is everywhere apparent. The
veracity is a product of the precision with which space and time are
handled, but that precision is bounded by an awareness of similitude.
Seen in earthly terms the spatio-temporal aspect of the journey is *like*
this, but only like: Time has its roots in the divine mind which is
immeasurable, and merely its leaves in those places and events
which are accessible to human measurement and description.

E come il tempo tegna in cotal testo
le sue radici e ne li altri le fronde,
omai a te puo esser manifesto.
                         (*Paradiso*, XXVII 118-20)

(And how time has its roots in that vessel, and in the others
its shoots, may now be clear to you.)

Bunyan allows himself much greater latitude than Dante in the
way in which he uses time. Though Christian's journey is in part
a vision, it is also an image for the passage through life of an
Everyman figure, and a dreamlike condensation of a whole spiritual
life. That is to say, it is visionary for us but literal for Christian,
while Dante's journey is vision for both him and his readers. As
Christian nears the Heavenly City he seems to be moving farther
and farther from the possibility of losing his way there, and from
losing his right of access to immortality. But the present moment
is always potentially the moment of salvation or damnation, and
thus eclipses both past and future in its intensity. ('Thou fool, *this*
night shall thy soul be required of thee.') This is made clear to the

Dreamer-Narrator when he sees Ignorance seeking access to the City immediately after Christian and Hopeful have entered in. Ignorance has had a much easier passage across the river of death than Christian; he was ferried over in the boat of Vainhope where Christian had only Hopeful to dissipate the 'horror of mind' and to help him keep his head above the waters. Ignorance is however refused entry into the City, and bound hand and foot:

> Then they took him up, and carried him through the air to
> the door that I saw in the side of the Hill, and put him
> in there. Then I saw that there was a way to Hell, even
> from the Gates of Heaven, as well as from the City of
> *Destruction*. So I awoke, and behold it was a Dream.
>
> (*Pilgrim's Progress*, p.163)

Time is one thing for Christian, and another for Ignorance: the reader has the benefit of experiencing both.

The passage of time in *Piers Plowman* is similarly controlled, very roughly, by the duration of the Dreamer's earthly life. Langland however uses several other kinds of time scale to diminish the importance of that single human scale: dream time, liturgical time, the cycle of the seasons (as in the passage dealing with the cultivation of the Half-Acre), and Christian historical time from the Creation to the coming of Anti-Christ. The juxtaposition and alternation of these various kinds of time is only replaced very briefly by complete interpenetration and simultaneity during the climactic sequence of events from the Crucifixion to the Harrowing of Hell. The several ways of measuring duration are an important and obviously carefully planned supplementary indication of the meaning of particular incidents, but the overall effect of their combination in the poem is of timelessness. The point in the poem at which the diverse time scales are concentrated together is a representation of those Christian events most purely historical and yet most absolutely out of time by virtue of being perpetually present to the believer. Eschatology, collective and personal morality, and the possibility of grace and redemption are all affected by, and dependent upon, the Crucifixion.

There is in *The Faerie Queene* no single theological event which can thus gather up the various strands of narrative. The adventures of the heroes continue simultaneously yet separately, with sporadic reminders of connection provided by references to a common allegiance to the Faerie Queene, and by the appearance in several narratives of the same characters. Spenser is not only diachronistic in his allusions to myth and chronicle, but also resolutely synchronistic. The sense of similar events occurring all over a series of similar landscapes is sometimes so strong that we suspect some characters of assuming the divine characteristic of being in two places at the same time. But Spenser is deliberately creating a sense of other time, non-time; this sense is an important component in our imaginative picture of a world which derives both its sometimes irritating vagueness and its intensity from not being subject to the same temporal criteria as our own.

Blurring of narrative time and sequence is one of the principal means by which Spenser creates the illusion of an a-temporal order of reality, but it is interesting to note that our sense of a-temporality is often strongest in the great set-pieces of the allegory, and these are independent of the main movement of the narrative. Calidore's vision of the dancing graces in Book VI, Canto x, is outside his real adventure: it is an intensified vision of pastoral rather than an experience of pastoral life. The accounts of the Garden of Adonis in Book III, Canto vi, and of the Temple of Venus in Book IV, Canto x, are both reported excursions into past history: the first is given by the narrator in the course of telling of Belphoebe's birth and upbringing, while the second occurs in Scudamour's account of how he won Amoret. Since these descriptions stand outside the sequence of the action, and are moreover essentially static, Spenser is not free to create a sense of the timelessness of these *loci* by defeating the reader's expectations of realistic spatio-temporal location (as he consistently does in the rest of the poem). But they are if anything even further beyond the human dimensions of space and duration. As with Calidore's vision, they are crystallizations of themes apparent elsewhere in *The Faerie Queene*, and their visionary quality stems not from vagueness, a deliberate refusal to tell the reader when and where events occurred and how long they took, but from lucidity and preciseness. Paradoxically, the Gardens of Adonis contain both the triumphs of time and of timelessness. 'Wicked *Time*'

> who with his scyth adresst,
> Does mow the flowring herbes and goodly things,

And all their glory to the ground downe flings. ...

is held in balance by the renewing power of Genius, who gives
fresh life to those whose 'mortall state' is ended.

> After that they againe returned beene,
>   They in that Gardin planted be againe;
>   And grow afresh, as they had neuer seene
>   Fleshly corruption, nor mortall paine.
>   Some thousand yeares so doen they there remaine;
>   And then of him are clad with other hew,
>   Or sent into the chaungefull world againe. ...
>   (III vi 39 and 33)

Genius's power is expressed in the person of Adonis, who is 'eterne
in mutabilitie,/And by succession made perpetuall'. Spenser gives
this landscape its particular quality by insisting on simultaneity:

> There is continuall spring, and haruest there
>   Continuall, both meeting at one time:
>   For both the boughes doe laughing blossomes beare,
>   And with fresh colours decke the wanton Prime,
>   And eke attonce the heauy trees they clime,
>   Which seeme to labour vnder their fruits lode. ...
>   (III vi 42)

The Garden of Adonis displays in a paradoxical and concentrated form a process common to many allegories: emphasis
on the co-existence of all the aspects and effects of time convinces
us that the allegorical world is outside it. The disruption of expectations of normal sequence and causality, and the deliberate
avoidance of realistic chronology, are other means by which the
same effect is achieved in allegories. 'Then', 'when', and 'while', are
in allegory frequently deprived of any adverbial precision.

In *The Castle* and *The Trial* Kafka uses both a disruption of
chronology and causality and also (in a characteristically inverted
way) the sense of past time. K.'s relationships with other characters
develop with extraordinary and elliptical speed, and the consequences of certain actions take effect with unpredictable rapidity.
The past imposes itself upon the present, although not as a source
of meaning and understanding, but of their opposites. K. is made

liable to the judgment 'Guilty' because of something he has done or which has happened in the past, but that past is as impenetrable to him as to the reader: it is the origin of threat and fallibility rather than of security and value. Kafka thus employed two standard allegorical procedures to achieve a standard allegorical effect. Even though the past functions in a way which denies both the accessibility and the value of tradition (a reversal of its function in earlier allegories), the worlds of *The Castle* and *The Trial* have that quality, characteristic of all the worlds of allegory, of not being subject to normal temporal and spatial conditions.

The sense of the past and the a-temporality of allegory derive equally from its foundation in the ideal and its didactic purpose. For both aesthetic and cognitive reasons, any abstraction that is rich in associations over a long period of time will obviously be more imaginatively potent, and thus appear more valuable, than one which is very firmly limited to one particular period. The basis of the allegorical action in ideals and abstractions imposes upon the author the obligation to reduce the sense of one single instant of time, or of a single succession of incidents – as he must also reduce the sense of a single limited visual entity. This has to happen if the reader's imagination is to be freed from the limitations of particularity, if he is to feel that the concepts have relevance for him as they do for the protagonists.

Spenser's treatment of the concept of love demonstrates the possibilities of a method whereby multiple associations, derived from various cultural and literary sources, interact. It also shows the didactic value of a disrupted and non-sequential narrative. We first learn of Amoret's birth in Book III, Canto vi. She is the twin sister of the chaste Belphoebe; their mother Chrysogyne fell asleep and was miraculously impregnated by the sun, and was delivered also in sleep. That their birth was 'of the wombe of morning dew' and their conception 'of the ioyous Prime' gives them both mythical and specifically Christian associations (the dew falling on Gideon's fleece is a standard typological image of the Virgin's conception of Christ). The two children are found by the companions of Diana, who adopts Belphoebe, while Venus takes Amoret as a substitute for Cupid who has 'strayd', and causes her to be brought up in her temple set in the Gardens of Adonis. In Canto ix of the same book Britomartis, the maiden warrior of chastity, finds Scudamour lamenting Amoret's imprisonment in the House of Busyrane, and subsequently delivers her from that power. In Book IV, Canto v, Amoret is the only woman able to wear the girdle of 'chast loue,/ And wiuehood true'; in Canto vii she is saved from rape and death by Belphoebe; and in Cantos viii and ix is under the protection of Prince Arthur. Canto x is Scudamour's account of entering the Temple of Venus and winning Amoret. A personification whose name is a diminutive of *amor* is thus given associations with the Incarnation, with the mythical power of the sun (Phoebus Apollo), and with various forms of chastity, militancy, and constancy. She is both a twin to the foster-child of Phoebe, and a superior substitute for Cupid; she is reared in the midst of a place of immortality and renewal; and the knight who claims her and her love bears a name which conflates the ideas of love, bravery, and defence. This rich and complex treatment of the abstraction 'love' would not have been possible had not Spenser ransacked the past, and treated his narrative present in an essentially digressive way. We are left not with the impression of a single concept personified, but of an intricate structure of associations clustering round the person of 'faire Amoret'.

Kafka's method of building up a series of associations round the single idea of 'the Law' is arguably the same as Spenser's in dealing with 'love'. Both are making it possible for their readers to possess something more than a wordish description or definition. The ideas are not limited to any single context either temporal or fictional; in the course of the allegory they become both grander and more multi-dimensional than either any intellectual definition or any one image in the allegory. It is very common to experience a sense of the increasingly massive nature of central concepts while reading an allegory, and this is related to the cumulative and trans-temporal way in which the action unfolds.

Angus Fletcher has said that the mode is both iconographically and dimensionally 'monumental' : this sums up very well the hieratic and traditional nature of so many allegories, and also its didactic and exhortatory qualities. It always has the weight of argument and demonstration behind it, but it is argument and demonstration beyond the demands of any particular situation political, theological, or intellectual. The impulse to write allegory and the forms of allegories themselves are deeply rooted in ideas and ideals; these are necessarily more amorphous than objects or persons, and thus more recalcitrant to both author and reader.

Consequently any allegory will sometimes seem unduly vague or cumbrous or antiquated to even the most dedicated of its readers. These vices are of course the result of attempting to present abstractions in a rich and complex way: lack of resonance is perhaps the antithetical vice of literature which concerns itself primarily with the particularity of objects and people.

Concepts, beliefs, and ideas do however have an extraordinary power to survive – they are the elements which give strength to all literary works, however 'mimetic' or 'realistic' their surface may be. Few of us now read the medieval Romances of Huon of Bordeaux or Guy of Warwick, which are concerned entirely with persons and actions; but we do read *Troilus and Criseyde*, which explores the ideals and beliefs that influence persons and their actions. Chaucer's poem has the power to move and please us because it narrates a particular story but is also concerned with concepts that are accessible to our experience as the particular story is not – with love, with mutability, with the power of human beings to choose between various kinds of alternative value. With these and other concepts allegory concerns itself: it could therefore be seen as a mode which focuses on and expresses those things that are most essential and perennial in literary works, while doing so in forms that are to a considerable degree independent of the exigencies of particular periods or genres.

The relative value of the particular and the general in literary works is Johnson's concern in a much-quoted passage in the *Preface to Shakespeare*; predictably, he comes down on the side of the general:

> Nothing can please many, and please long, but just
> representations of general nature. Particular manners can be
> known to few, and therefore few only can judge how
> nearly they are copied. The irregular combinations of fanciful
> invention may delight a-while, by that novelty of which
> the common satiety of life sends us all in quest; but the
> pleasures of sudden wonder are soon exhausted, and
> the mind can only repose on the stability of truth.

These alternatives are simultaneously present in allegory, which offers us both the 'sudden wonder' of 'irregular combinations of fanciful invention' and the repose of the mind 'on the stability of truth'.

2 Limitations: the idea of order as delight or threat

Beneath the freedom and essential enigma in the handling of central concepts in many allegories, the emphasis on their existence out of time, lies a belief in the possibility of pattern revealing itself in variousness. The several strands of the narrative, and the multiplex figures and images which provide texture and meaning locally, anatomize the concepts and emotions and beliefs which concern the author. Particular events or places then provide a culmination to this process. They focus through metaphor and so have the essential open-endedness intrinsic to that figure, but by virtue of providing a culmination, a focus, imply the possibility of perceiving coherence in the world, and the viability of a total conception of life. The values and structures revealed are natural components of an interpreted world.

This is the point on which allegories of the past two centuries most obviously part company with their predecessors : it will have become increasingly obvious that throughout this argument examples were preponderantly drawn from pre-eighteenth-century allegories. Seen historically, the mode displays continuity of method but discontinuity of purpose.

Even if Kafka's *method* of presenting the Castle or the concept of the Law resembles Spenser's in his presentation of central places or concepts (like Love), even if both the worlds of *The Trial* and *The Faerie Queene* are ambiguous, ironic, and independent of realistic spatio-temporal restraints and causality, there remains an immense difference. The conclusions the reader arrives at in the act of interpreting Kafka's works, the sort of relationship they posit between themselves and whatever reality the reader inhabits, are almost antithetical to those of the great earlier allegories. In *The Trial*, *The Castle*, his short stories – in the overwhelming majority of modern narratives using allegorical methods – ambiguity moves towards doubt, towards denial of the possibility of meaning independent of but shared by author, hero, and reader; in *The Faerie Queene*, in common with most allegories until the eighteenth century, ambiguity generates certainty, conviction, the affirmation of meaning and value.

Spenser's narrative is fantastic, overtly so; Kafka's are superficially realistic, even mundane. But at the end we ask ourselves : '*Is* there any such thing as "the Law"?' We have no doubt, reading

Spenser with sympathy, that Love (in a very extensive definition of the term) *does* exist. K.'s feelings, his fear, his sense of being threatened and exhausted, are intensely real, but are the things that inspire those feelings real? Are they even actually and demonstrably evil as Archimago, or Acrasia, or Lady Munera are? Many modern writers – and Melville in *Moby Dick* is a good instance of this – use the ornate imagery, the multiple action, the rhetorical gestures toward meaning which engage our interpretative energies, only to leave us with the sense that the centre is void. Medieval and renaissance allegorists create a series of interlocking and overlapping circles, but there at the centre is the image or event which asserts value even while eluding definition: Dante's multifoliate Rose in the *Paradiso*, the Harrowing of Hell, the entry into the Heavenly City, the destruction of the Dragon.

The physical quality of the central images vividly suggests this divergence between earlier and modern allegories: like the 'huge hill,/Cragged, and steep' on which Truth stands in the Donne Satyre, the Tower of Truth '*high* to the East' in *Piers Plowman*, the Rose in its rose-garden in *Le Roman de la Rose*, Mount Acidale in Book VI of *The Faerie Queene*, the House Beautiful and the Delectable Mountains from which the Heavenly City can be seen, all command the landscape, the heroes' visual field, and the reader's belief in perceptible value. By contrast the maëlstrom (in Poe and in the final wreck of the Pequod), the frozen and trackless ice which is the setting for the confrontation between the Baron and the Monster and for the final climax of the drama in *Frankenstein*, the labyrinths of Kafka, the faceless and squalid urban architecture of *1984* – these are not things upon which we can focus, but engulfing, pervasive, threatening in their blankness and endless repetitiveness.

Many works of the nineteenth and twentieth centuries have the ambiguity, the multivalence, the 'polysemous' texture of allegory: arguably many of the very greatest – Melville's *Moby Dick*, Proust's *A la Recherche du temps perdu*, Joyce's *Ulysses* and *Finnegans Wake*, Mann's *Doctor Faustus* and *The Magic Mountain*. They are also characteristically allegorical in offering continuous commentary upon the action and in being mythopoeic: the narrative consciously re-enacts recurrent mythic or legendary patterns. These are most often patterns of obsession, isolation, and possession by an *idée fixe* or compulsion, and thus typically 'modern' in their concentration on the situation of the individual – though, as Fletcher suggests, all allegorical heroes are to some extent dæmonically possessed and compulsive. The mythopoeic quality is apparent despite varieties of narrative style and subject-matter: Swann like Orpheus searching the darkening boulevards for the elusive Odette-Eurydice, an analogy of the narrator's attempt to possess Albertine and of Charlus's to retain power over Charlie Morel; Ahab questing for the White Whale, a quest which also defines and asserts his own identity; Bloom surrounded by echoes of the classical world of Ulysses; Leverkühn in his metaphysical, metavenereal Faustus-pact with the enemy, granted in the twenty-fifth chapter 'a whole houre-glasseful of divel-time, genius-time', ... 'high-flying time, full twenty-four years *ab dato recessi*'. Mann gives a historical dimension to the Faust metaphor by the analogy between the composer's life and the course of German history, and the comments of the narrator, Zeitblom, make this explicit: 'the fantastic mingles with the horrible: up to the very end the crudely legendary, the grim deposit of saga in the soul of the nation is invoked, with all its familiar echoes and reverberations.' But in these works multiplicity of perceptions has replaced multiplicity of meanings. Always we are made aware that when moral coherence or hierarchy or teleology appears to be there it originates in a perceiver (Ishmael, Marcel, Zeitblom), not in the nature of reality.

The characteristic procedures of earlier allegories are thus present in a great number of modern works; but if the formal connections are clear the ideological and metaphysical dimensions are very different, and the question remains – 'Why?' The difference emerges most obviously in the contrasting treatments of order and system: an examination of these will serve as a preliminary to the answers offered tentatively in the final section.

Spenser's Mutabilitie Cantos, the unfinished Book VII of *The Faerie Queene*, are concerned precisely with pattern emerging from variousness and with the order that underlies change and particularity. The dramatized debate presents arguments for and against the assertion that the only immutable law ordering the universe is the law of change. The Titaness Mutability complains that Jove and the Gods 'Arrogate to themselues ambitiously' the sovereignty of the world, and claims this power as hers. The earth

> only seemes vnmov'd and permanent,
> And vnto *Mutability* not thrall;

Yet is she chang'd in part, and eeke in generall.

For, all that from her springs, and is ybredde,
   How-euer fayre it flourish for a time,
   Yet see we soone decay; and, being dead,
   To turne again vnto their earthly slime:
   Yet, out of their decay and mortall crime,
   We daily see new creatures to arize;
   And of their Winter spring another Prime,
   Vnlike in forme, and chang'd by strange disguise:
So turne they still about, and change in restlesse wise.

(VII vii 17-18)

The case of Mutability rests on the fact that the transformations of the material world are more certain and demonstrable than any supposed metaphysical purpose directing those transformations. This certainty makes the law of change superior to any other, and she, as goddess of change, is therefore superior to any other deity. Mutability asserts that Nature, the arbiter in the debate, should support her claims, and demands that Nature summon before the assembly all the times and seasons of the year as proof that all is dominated by change. There follows a procession of the four seasons, the twelve months with their signs of the Zodiac, Day and Night, the Hours, and lastly Life and Death; all are summoned to appear by Order, acting as a kind of Master of the Revels.

Mutability makes a final claim for her right to dominion.

For, who sees not, that *Time* on all doth pray?
But *Times* do change and moue continually.
So nothing here long standeth in one stay:

(VII vii 47)

She concludes that her right to power is based upon laws of Nature:

Then since within this wide great *Vniuerse*
   Nothing doth firme and permanent appeare,
   But all things tost and turned by transuerse:
   What then should let, but I aloft should reare
   My Trophee, and from all the triumph beare?

(VII vii 56)

Nature however gives judgment against Mutability, and supports
the power of Jove on the grounds that though all things hate stead-
fastness, they are nevertheless subjected to rules even in their
changing. It is interesting to note that the rules are determined by
the nature of things themselves, and not imposed upon them; they
are organic rather than mechanic rules.

> They are not changed from their first estate;
> But by their change their being doe dilate:
> And turning to themselues at length againe,
> Doe worke their owne perfection so by fate:
> Then ouer them Change doth not rule and raigne;
> But they raigne over change, and doe their states maintaine.

(VII vii 58)

The substance of this argument is to be found in numerous medieval
allegories, from the *De Consolatione Philosophiae* of Boethius
onwards: it reappears in Alain de Lille's *De Planctu Naturae*, in *Le
Roman de la Rose*, in the work of Chaucer, Gower, and Christine de
Pisan. Spenser shows that he is aware of working in a literary and
allegorical tradition by referring the reader to Chaucer's presentation of Nature in the *Parlement of Foules* and Alain de Lille's in
the *De Planctu Naturae*. Mutability is the principle of change; in
the more capricious guise of Fortune she affects the revolutions of
human life. What is interesting in Spenser's presentation of this
concept is its elasticity, its freedom from either rigidity of control
or lawlessness of operation. 'Immutable' does not suggest a boring
fixity, and the 'earthly slime' to which things inevitably return is
a womb as much as a grave. Spenser adds a reflective comment
of his own on the debate:

> Then gin I thinke on that which Nature sayd,
>   Of that same time when no more *Change* shall be,
> But stedfast rest of all things firmely stayd
> Vpon the pillours of Eternity,
>   That is contrayr to *Mutabilitie*:
> For all that moueth, doth in *Change* delight:
> But thence-forth all shall rest eternally. ....

(VII viii 2)

This is a view of the world in which a certain kind of allegory could
thrive. All the verbs used of the action of things in changing suggest

energy; they 'dilate', turn to themselves, 'worke their owne perfection', 'maintain their states'. It is directed energy, even as the protagonists in all allegories are energies directed by their authors, whether to expound, to demonstrate, or simply to delight. The powers of intelligent observation, both of the natural world and of the actions of men, contribute to an awareness of the abstract principles creating an essentially benevolent kind of order.

Though Spenser formulates the argument in humanistic rather than exclusively Christian terms, for example using 'Jove' for God, the claim that things 'Doe worke their owne perfection so by fate' suggests the Christian doctrine that figures are validated by their fulfilment. According to this, things in the natural world are 'perfected' only by some supra-temporal process; on this assumption rests the allegorical interpretation of the Bible. Auerbach discusses this conception of history as evolving according to divine plan in the essay 'Figura', and also uses it in criticizing the *Divine Comedia*, in *Mimesis* (1957). In the *Inferno*, Farinata and Cavalcante are given tragic dimension by the fact that their most characteristic qualities have become dominant, but dominant in that world beyond time, Hell, where there is no possibility of their fulfilling the desires towards which these characteristics impel them. Their being is dilated, turned again to that which is most themselves, and they are fixed so in eternity. This could be called the negative side of ordered mutability; its positive aspect is shown in the interpretation of events in Biblical history as representing some subsequent divine happening. For example, Jonah in the belly of the whale is seen as a prefiguration of Christ's entombment and descent into Hell. Whatever the particular details of an event (Jonah was after all running away from God) it possesses a secondary meaning by virtue of its place in a wider temporal and moral order.

Such beliefs in the teleology of natural and temporal processes in the universe become less and less accessible to writers, and attitudes to order change as the definition of it becomes contracted and more materialistic. Even from a casual reading it is clear that works of an allegorical nature from the late seventeenth century onwards, far from offering an ordered universe as an object of delighted contemplation, are conceived in a spirit hostile (sometimes violently so) to any attempted systematization of life. They are still frequently concerned with order, but as something threatening. Regulation is no longer a matter of the ordering of the seasons

or the spheres, but the circumscription of people's lives by various
codifications of behaviour: as in 'the Regulations'. In the work of
Swift, in the partially allegorical *1984* and *Brave New World* there
recurs a suspicion of order, of system, of any kind of hierarchy.
If we compare the scene in which Piers the Ploughman directs the
labours of the Pilgrims in the Half-Acre with the organized drudgery
of the animals in *Animal Farm*, this change is made very clear. The
Half-Acre field is a figure both for the individual soul and for the
secular community and the community of the Church. Its cultivation, over which Piers exercises strict control, represents both
the disciplining of the soul in order to attain its spiritual needs, and
the regulation of society to achieve its material and spiritual needs.
By contrast, the Stakhanovian labours of the animals are a kind of
slavery, only made absurd rather than tragic by the Aesopian form.
It is impossible to think that Orwell saw the condition of Russians
under Stalin as absurd.

Swift is in many ways a crucial transitional figure in the development of allegory. He is immersed in its techniques, but his work has
qualities in common both with classic allegories and those of the
post-Romantic period. As we might expect, his attitude to order is
thoroughly ambiguous. On the one hand he appears to distrust
intellectual, artistic, and metaphysical systems, while on the other
the carefully ordered society of the Houyhnhnms comes in for at
least moderate approbation. The Houyhnhnms avoid all emotion,
maintain the level of population exactly, have no history, no
diseases, no fear of dying, and condition their young to do and be
exactly the same. This state is achieved by the rule of Reason,
rather than by conditioning, but it offers a close parallel to that of
the inhabitants of the World State in Huxley's *Brave New World*.
It is impossible to say how far this was Utopia for Swift, though it
is for Gulliver. The voyage to the Houyhnhnms is in part a pretext
for another attack on Yahoo/Man, disorderly, bad-tempered, and
above all, stinking of shit (as Orwell put it, another excuse for Swift
to shout at his fellow creatures 'You are filthier than you are!').

Whether or not Swift saw the frigid orderliness of the
Houyhnhnms as desirable, other parts of *Gulliver's Travels* certainly
show contempt for art, science, literature, and music. These, though
disciplines in themselves, are of course vehicles for personal expression and individual enthusiasm. All of them are suppressed by the
conditioning classes in Huxley's world after Ford, and by the élite

in *1984*, as constituting a threat to a controlled society (as any history of censorship under repressive régimes suggests that indeed they do). The paradox in Swift's work is that a distaste for individualism and eccentric enthusiasms is coupled with a curiously all-embracing utilitarianism – which causes him to attack systems with any kind of metaphysical basis. The problem is that Swift is capable of attacking on both sides of an argument; he appears reluctant to accept a world that is ordered, but diverse, changing, and open to individual curiosity and imagination. Johnson's comment that imagination, 'a licentious and vagrant faculty, unsusceptible of limitations, and impatient of restraint, has always endeavoured to baffle the logician, to perplex the confines of distinction, and burst the inclosures of regularity' seems to define Swift's fears. It is the problem of the realist and pessimist – if one allows people the liberty to burst the enclosures of regularity they are inevitably going to abuse it; but any system set up to govern or direct them or give them moral purpose has the same corrupt source: man.

   Where this distrust of systems most appears is in the contemptuous account of Laputa, but throughout *Gulliver's Travels* and *A Tale of a Tub* there is a suspiciousness of intellectual and imaginative pursuits that lack practical application. The actions of Martin, the brother who represents the Anglican church in *A Tale of a Tub*, are approved entirely on practical grounds. The acute consciousness of material things that contributes so much to the satirical effect of some passages in Swift's work, also makes for the philistine dismissal of pursuits that are not strictly material. The Academy of Projectors in Lagado is shown as not only ridiculous but sinister, because of the ways in which it attempts to control intelligence, to make people less conscious and curious (as they are in the totalitarian states of *Brave New World* and *1984*). But the Houyhnhnms are exactly that: incurious. They have eliminated ambiguity in their language, as does Newspeak (and would presumably regard allegory with incredulity, since they 'have not the least idea of books or literature'). Their response to anything outside the limits of their own experience is polite but dismissive scepticism. In *Gulliver's Travels* and *A Tale of a Tub*, reason is not Ratio, the medieval personification of the supreme faculty to infer logical conclusions from observed phenomena, but common sense – that which makes us accept the obvious, and avoid extremes of behaviour. In short, it is that 'commune sence' which Spenser thought was pandered to by literary plainness. Despite its ambiguities, Swift's view of order is altogether a more cautious and narrow one than that found in the Mutabilitie Cantos. For Swift, as for Langland, most man-made systems are corrupt and flawed; but for him, unlike Langland, there are no alternative hierarchies which can be invoked.

In 1984 the power élite has constructed a society systematically designed to eliminate all personal privacy, liberty, and flights of imagination (i.e., all non-conformist deviation). In *Brave New World*, technological 'advance' has been used to create a pre-determined world which is rebarbative because any possibility of change has been eradicated. The castes, Alpha, Beta, Gamma, Delta, Epsilon-moron, are each in immutable slots. Admittedly Huxley cheats by emphasizing the conditioning of sexual response and the control of population: both areas in which even the most thoroughly conditioned among us most wish to retain the illusions of freedom, choice, and individuality. Relying on an emotional response to the sexual climate in the New World, he evades responsibility for any close analysis of the circumstances and objectives of the political control which is the root cause of that climate. A particular genetic aristocracy benefits from the stability and solidarity of the World State. These qualities are repeatedly emphasized; the motto of the World State is 'Community, Identity, Stability'; Bokanovsky's Process, by which nearly a hundred identical beings can be produced from a single fertilized egg, is a 'major instrument of social stability'. The resident Controller for Western Europe, Mustapha Mond, observes to the Savage that 'It isn't only art that's incompatible with happiness; it's also science. Science is dangerous; we have to keep it most carefully chained and muzzled' (p.177). This is because freely developing experimental science is capable of disrupting any controlled order. The Savage, whose vocabulary and moral responses are based almost entirely on the plays of Shakespeare, is the allegorical representative of a society in which choice and change are intrinsic elements. Though many of Huxley's novels contain characters that are little more than typed representatives of certain attitudes, the Savage is probably the most allegorical in function, both because of the nature of his character and because of the fictional narrative in which it operates. His suicide represents the final eradication of choice and personal responsibility, and of the moral view of the world consequent upon these.

Mustapha Mond points out that tragedies are impossible without social instability :

> The world's stable now. People are happy, they get what
> they want, and they never want what they can't get. They're
> well-off; they're safe; they're never ill; they're not afraid of
> death; they're blissfully ignorant of passion and old age;
> they're plagued with no mothers or fathers; they've got no
> wives, or children, or loves to feel strongly about; they're
> so conditioned that they practically can't help behaving as
> they ought to behave.   (p.173)

This 'stedfast rest of all things firmly stayd' is presented by Huxley as morally and aesthetically negative, and in a way his conclusions are the predictable ones of the liberal intellectual (Orwell's too?) – politically desirable ends like the cure of poverty seem less desirable when a concomitant is the erosion of individual liberty. It may be that at periods when stability seems unattainable in human communities, as in the Middle Ages or the Renaissance, it can be contemplated with pleasure as a Divine attribute. When it comes to seem not only materially attainable but imminent, it appears repulsive. Order is no longer a component in the harmony of the cosmos, but a weapon in the hands of necessarily corruptible men.

In the belief that it is possible to construct a 'single, complex, harmonious mental Model of the Universe', earlier allegories offer close parallels to the visual arts. The frescoes of Santa Maria Novella, those in the Palazzo della Ragione at Padua (Il Salone), the capitals of the Doges' palace, countless medieval illuminations, all show an allegorized iconography of order. In Il Salone, the Planets, their children, the Seven Liberal Arts, the signs of the Zodiac, and the Labours of the Months are organized into patterned mutual relationships. In frescoes, horizontal divisions can be used to emphasize the hieratic quality of the vision. In the *Bibles Moralisées*, in the devotional treatises such as the *Somme Le Roy*, the illuminations order the moral world by establishing elaborate parallels between different types and eras. In the *Maestà* by Duccio at Siena, the restraint with which each scene is presented in an almost theatrical setting serves to draw attention to the way in which certain events are related to each other; subtle repetitions and echoes of gesture and grouping are apparent because of the discipline with which colour is used, and with which the setting of an event is suggested.

There is a marked contrast to such art in the eighteenth-century concern with the sublime, the picturesque, the Gothick, and subsequently in the anarchic quality of the images which delighted Romantic painters. And a complementary shift of taste occurs in music – especially in the development of opera – in the search for more expressive and emotionally mimetic forms. The eighteenth century is a transitional period both for the changes in allegory and in the conception of order. Pope's *Essay on Man* and *The Dunciad* combine an intellectual assertion of order with a profound emotional fascination with disorder – a combination perhaps most apparent in the tensions of the passage describing the advent of the empire of Dullness and Chaos:

> Thus at her felt approach, and secret might,
> *Art* after *Art* goes out, and all is Night.
> See skulking *Truth* to her old Cavern fled,
> Mountains of Casuistry heap'd o'er her head!
> *Philosophy*, that leaned on Heav'n before,
> Shrinks to her second cause, and is no more.
> *Physic* of *Metaphysic* begs defence,
> And *Metaphysic* calls for aid on *Sense!*
> See *Mystery* to *Mathematics* fly!
> In vain! they gaze, turn giddy, rave, and die.
> *Religion* blushing veils her sacred fires,
> And unawares *Morality* expires.
> For *public* Flame, nor *private*, dares to shine;
> Nor *human* Spark is left, nor Glimpse *divine!*
> Lo! thy dread Empire, CHAOS! is restor'd;
> Light dies before thy uncreating word:
> Thy hand, great Anarch! lets the curtain fall;
> And Universal Darkness buries All.
> (Dunciad, iv 639-56)

3 Some historical influences and their effect on allegory

The allegorical mode survives after the end of the seventeenth century, while serving very different purposes. In a sense what happens is that allegory goes underground: from being the advocate of conventional social values, or at least of a conservative kind of wisdom, it tends to become subversive, satirical, and concerned with the predicament of the rebel and the outsider. Allegories become scarcer or more covert after the end of the seventeenth century; those works which are allegorical seem to be increasingly critical or even hostile towards the conventions and structures of society. These conventions are shown as threatening rather than supporting the heroes. While the Court of the Faerie Queene, Gloriana, is never directly described by Spenser, it is a still point, a source of moral virtue and strength to the knights as they are sent out from it and return to it. By contrast, the Court of the Law in *The Trial* is a vague but perpetually imminent menace for Joseph K. The allegorical action in modern works is at once more obscure, in the sense that it is almost impossible to ascertain its ultimate meaning, and at the same time allusions to mythology, history, theology, become less frequent as allegories lose their confident encyclopaedism, their role as books of knowledge and counsel, and become more exclusively personal Odysseys. *1984*, or *Der Steppenwolf*, or *The Trial* (however different as allegories), all assert personal choice and subjective evaluation against collective or cosmic systems. There is sometimes the sense that their authors attempt to make us accept the secondary implications of the stories through bafflement and fear rather than through curiosity or the desire for wisdom.

Clearly, a growing antipathy to systematization cannot be the sole reason for these changes. It is even doubtful whether this antipathy is itself causal rather than symptomatic. Edwin Honig suggests in *Dark Conceit* that:

> Some explanation for the elusive pattern and the increasing
> ambiguity in modern allegories may be found in the destruction
> of the rigid base of cultural authority upon which allegory
> traditionally depended, and in the relatively greater stress put
> on the autonomy of the artist since the Reformation.

This needs some modification — modern allegories are not really more ambiguous though they direct ambiguity to different ends; earlier ones do not depend upon a 'rigid base of cultural authority' so much as upon a consensus of beliefs, philosophical and metaphysical givens about the nature of the world and the relationship of literature to it. Modern allegories have their philosophical commonplaces too. Honig none the less isolates two of the most important areas in which we can begin to find reasons for the changes in allegory. His second, the autonomy of the artist, is as relevant to critics' responses to allegory during this century and the last as it is to the features of allegory itself.

Since Coleridge (and ultimately Goethe) allegory has been the loser in a symbol versus allegory competition: meaning is seen as being actually and naturally there in symbol, but artificially there in allegory. Hazlitt, Coleridge, Yeats, and countless of their contemporaries and inheritors assume that allegory is a matter of imposition: it curbs the freedom of the writer and imposes on the reader to the point of bullying or boredom. The autonomy of the individual whether as maker or receiver is necessarily threatened by it. Baudelaire stands apart from his contemporaries in observing that system-making is a natural intellectual activity and not *per se* the monopoly of any particular society or literary form, even though he shares with them the emotional stance that associates system with *damnation* and *châtiment*:

> Un système est une espèce de damnation qui nous pousse à une abjuration perpétuelle; il en faut toujours inventer un autre, et cette fatigue est un cruel châtiment.

A suspicion of regulated ways of life, a disbelief in the possibility of complex metaphysical schemata which might have absolute value, seem to be associated with various features of the intellectual history of the period from the mid-seventeenth century: these obviously affect all literature and art and not allegory alone. First, the growth of a materialist ethic not unconnected with certain aspects of Puritan thought; second, the individualism of the Romantic period; and third, the increasing internalization of value, most obvious in Freudian and post-Freudian psychology, but with antecedents long before the end of the nineteenth century.

In *Religion and the Rise of Capitalism*, R. H. Tawney has discussed the interaction between a developing Puritan ethic and the evolution of mercantilist/capitalist economic systems. What emerges from this study is the extent to which an individualistic materialism governed the conduct of public affairs in England from about the 1640s onwards. It cannot, of course, be argued that Puritanism is the sole source of this; in the context of European societies, bourgeois anti-clericalism seems to have produced rather similar results, despite the Counter-Reformation. For a Puritan, the relationship of an individual with God is a matter of secret and solitary communion, and the world external to that relationship is hostile and peopled by enemies. In this world, however, it is his bounden duty to labour. Since the older virtues of prudence, patience, and diligence conveniently coincide with profit, the energetic pursuit of business can be justified as the fulfilment of God's will. Bunyan himself was aware that the argument that duty was spiritually profitable could be perniciously extended to justify the pursuit of profit as a duty. Mr Gripeman and his followers, inhabitants of the market-town of Love-Gain in the County of Coveting, argue just this; Faithful is arrested and put to death in Vanity Fair, a community based on the extortionate exchange of merchandise. In the climate of such thinking, fulfilling secular and material obligations can seem more moral than fulfilling spiritual and immaterial ones. In *The Tradesman's Calling* (1684), Richard Steele commented that friars and monks

> live only to themselves and to their formal devotion, but do
> employ themselves in no one thing to forward their own
> subsistence ... yet have the confidence to boast of this their
> course as a state of perfection; which in very deed, as to the
> worthiness of it, falls short of the poorest cobbler, for his
> is a calling of God, and theirs is none.

Many aspects of materialism, including the idealization of action at the expense of contemplation, obviously influence allegorical writing.

Religious individualism was one element that imperceptibly encouraged an individualist morality which valued personal effort and attainment more highly than the social fabric as a whole. Among the consequences of such a morality are changing attitudes to poverty. The poor are no longer to be pitied and aided, nor even seen as having the close connection with sanctity that they had for Langland and other medieval writers, by virtue of Christ's redemption of the world in the person of a poor man. The classic medieval doctrine, no matter how far from general practice, was that the relief of need is a primary obligation for those with means, because property was seen as stewardship and not just as a source of income. But between 1660 and 1760 a number of writers treat poverty and unemployment as evidencing sinfulness rather than misfortune. In *Giving Alms no Charity* (1704) Defoe denounces the 'luxury, pride, and sloth' of the new industrial proletariat. Few people pointed out that many labourers were forced out of a job by the enclosures; and those who did were fighting a losing battle. Consequently, the history of the Poor Laws in the eighteenth and nineteenth centuries reveals a conviction that relief should not just relieve, but deter. The needs of mere labourers are viewed as the result of 'individual improvidence and vice' (the words are those of the Poor Law Commissioners of 1834) by the property-owning classes in ages which worship property as the basis of social order. What the poor needed was 'regulation', best achieved by making them work under supervision, that of an employer who can control their labours. This has certain imaginative consequences which are relevant to the fortunes of allegory. For example, the concept of Time, an immensely fertile, if sometimes terrifying, concept during the Middle Ages and the Renaissance, is changed and narrowed by the application of mercantile ethics. Even among the uneducated of earlier periods for whom the remote personification of an abstraction would have held little immediacy, time was commonly defined as the time taken to perform a particular action: 'pissing while', 'paternoster while', day-break to sunset, or the months and seasons with their particular labours. It now becomes something that can be bought and sold, the principle according to which a man's life can be controlled by an employer. A correlative of the attitudes frequently shown to the poor can be seen in the contempt shown towards unsuccessful writers. Those who starve in a garret because what they write will not sell are violating their duty to labour in the production of what the majority will consume; their sufferings are therefore merited.

The assumptions and values which govern social morality and institutions from the later part of the seventeenth century onwards thus incorporate a considerable degree of materialist individualism; the effects of this are perhaps most apparent after the Industrial Revolution. The examples of order of system, and of conventional morality which confront writers, come to have unpleasant connotations of control and repression. The novel, which the Goncourts see as becoming

... la grande forme sérieuse, passionnée, vivante de l'étude littéraire

et de l'enquête sociale ... par l'analyse et par la recherche
psychologique, l'Histoire morale contemporaine. ...

(*Germinie Lacerteux*, Preface, 1864)

is as influential and widespread a form in the nineteenth century as
allegory was during the Middle Ages. But all those novelists who
attempt an informed and intelligent analysis of the sort of order
that governs the human condition come out against it rather than
for it. Zola's Rougon-Macquart novels offer a clear example; in
these his technical knowledge and understanding of the functioning
of industry and commerce are used to construct an indictment, not
an apologia. Even Dickens, who is naïve in his understanding of
the mechanisms of bureaucracy and trade, gave definitive form to
the hostile caricature of them in the Circumlocution Office and
Chancery, and in the rack-renting activities of the patriarchal Mr
Casby. However restrictive and repressive medieval and renaissance
social institutions may have been, they were inefficiently so.
Owners and rulers could not yet call on bureaucracy, the law, or
technology to support them. And before everybody, both rich and
poor, controllers and controlled, there was always one alternative,
immaterial, perfected system. In fact, it was rarely conceived as
being entirely alternative, since the immaterial was infused throughout the created world. However fictional the basis of theocratic order
may be, it nevertheless incorporates all the spiritual and imaginative
perfections that can be predicated of the Divine.

Certain cultural changes subsequent to the period extending from
the Middle Ages to the seventeenth century were also connected, if
not causally, with the pervasiveness of certain Protestant ways of
thought. These changes were in a large measure inimical to allegory,
at least to allegory of the kind written in the previous period. Not
least important was the view that created nature is an object of
suspicion, except perhaps in the course of scientific enquiry. D. A.
Traversi, writing on *Piers Plowman* for *Scrutiny*, contrasted the
creatural basis of Langland's imagination with the 'puritan intellec-
tualism' of Spenser. Though an oversimplification, it is true that
Langland passes easily from the material to the conceptual, as if
confident that they do not constitute separate orders of reality,
while in *The Faerie Queene* the meaning or significance of an event
is marginally more distant from the literal level of action. This is
not a purely Protestant versus Catholic division, since we can find

both kinds of writing at entirely Catholic or entirely Protestant periods, and in entirely secular works. C. S. Lewis, contrasting *Le Roman de la Rose* with the works of Chrétien de Troyes, made the obvious but often disregarded point that some medieval allegorists are much more realistic than other poets writing superficially 'realistic' Romances.

> ... the whole truth about Guillaume is missed until we see that he is more of a realist than Chrétien. ... In other words, the 'concrete' places and people in Chrétien are mere romantic supposals: the 'abstract' places and people in the *Romance of the Rose* are presentations of actual life.
>
> (*Allegory of Love*, p.115)

Nevertheless, if we take the terms of Traversi's comparison as having historical rather than purely religious significance, they are very suggestive. Lewis also observed, again in *The Allegory of Love* (pp.322-4), that 'all allegories whatever are likely to seem Catholic to the general reader', and suggested that this is related to the fact that Catholic theology tends to present the physical as some kind of symbol for the metaphysical. By contrast, some Protestant thinkers view the material world more as the habitation of the Flesh and the Devil, than as a source of delight, the greatest creation of the Divine Mind. This results in a sternly dismissive attitude to created nature, and sometimes also to literature which expresses moral and metaphysical truths through images drawn from worldly experience. (Eliot's comment on the 'dissociation of sensibility' which sets in after the Metaphysicals is pertinent here.) The allegorist must hold in balance *sens* and *matière*, the significance and the story. The latter is the material in which meaning is 'incorporated', given imaginable corporeal form. It will be difficult for him to do this if one half of the equation has been devalued from the start.

The growing materialism which contributes to the development of a certain kind of commercial and social ethic has correlations in the intellectual field. With the rise of natural science, entailing the precise analysis of natural conditions, based on observation, experiment, and calculation, mathematics and physics were raised to a new importance. In his Preface to the *Discourses Upon Trade* (1691) Sir Dudley North observed that 'Knowledge is in great measure become mechanical'. Swift's antipathy to non-practical intellectual activities and enquiry is thus in accord with the intellectual tendencies dominant in his environment.

During the Romantic period literature exhibits certain tendencies apparently less hostile to allegory – a delight in fantasy, in the remote and strange, and in exotic or antique cultures as a fertile source of imaginative materials rather than as normative models. But the emphasis on the individual, and on personal experience, which are also commonplaces in Romantic writing, preclude these tendencies from finding expression in allegories like *La Divina Commedia*, *Le Roman de la Rose*, or *The Faerie Queene*. Allegories such as those need some collective values, and also images which are collectively accessible. Modern allegories substitute the individual consciousness for shared values and for belief in external hierarchies, and in doing so distance themselves from the material in which abstractions are best expressed: objective phenomena and literary and philosophical traditions.

In *On Liberty*, John Stuart Mill claims that 'society has now fairly got the better of individuality; and the danger which threatens human nature is not the excess, but the deficiency, of personal impulses'. But in the emphasis on individualism Romantic writers were the legatees of Puritanism as much as Capitalists or Utilitarians (however much they would have hated that idea). In Romantic writing the supremacy of the private world is emphasized again and again, even as it is in Puritan spirituality. Nature and the created world are explored by the Imagination in order to discover a topography of the subjective: their value is that they constitute the material from which the individual vision or intense experience is derived. Coleridge assesses the economics of vitality solipsistically in 'Dejection: an Ode':

O Lady! we receive but what we give
And in our life alone does Nature live.

Emphasis on the individual and the value of his experience leads naturally to a very high estimate of originality, and a self-conscious, if not occasionally ridiculous, pursuit of that attribute.

The principal aims of an allegorist cannot be originality and subjectivity, though he may attain these as incidental felicities. First, he is concerned with abstractions, with universals, which by their linguistic nature must be comprehensible in so diverse a range of contexts as almost to give them objective status. Second, he is concerned to demonstrate these in terms accessible to any number of interested readers: truth may be difficult of access but it cannot be inaccessible. Finally, since he is generally interested in a complicated process, he needs an immense range of material to offer the expressive terms for the naked abstraction. If as well as being imaginative, the objectives of a work are social (to 'fashion a gentleman or noble person'), then subjectivity and originality, in the sense of the work being quite unlike anything written before, are hindrances. They prevent the general application of a particular narrative from being seen. The allegorist needs a diversity of images which have associations other than those attributed by the writer, as well as values susceptible to testing on a common pulse. His immediate social or religious aims may appear élitist, but if his work is to have the status of anything more than mere sectarian or class apologetics its values must correspond to generally held beliefs about the model of the world. And to retain any appeal when that model is no longer acceptable, an allegory must allow us to generate our own analogous models through its range of reference and suggestion. The general application of such reference is severely limited by an individualistic philosophy.

The growth of the European reading public occurring slowly in the eighteenth century and more rapidly in the nineteenth extended the audience of literature. One might suppose that this would have made at least some collective values accessible to writers. However, contempt for the taste of the general public became almost a commonplace among late Romantics, perhaps because the extended reading public consisted largely of those most benefiting from materialist economic and social systems, the property-owning and employing middle-classes. Writers, many of them seeing themselves as the chief defenders of the values of the individual, are likely to feel very much outside such systems. Consequently, they will be equally likely to disparage the values and tastes of people who are more obviously dependent upon the benefits and controls of industrial society. The Preface of the de Goncourt brothers' *Germinie Lacerteux*, written in 1864 (part of which has been quoted above (pp.119-20)), is an example of such disparagement. When works were intended for a Christian clerisy, a princely patron, or an aristocratic minority it was almost impossible for the writer to view his audience with contempt. But it becomes possible and even desirable when the writer is confronting an amorphous and anonymous public whose aesthetic and social premisses he is unlikely to share. He can afford to provoke hostility or suppression, since they at least constitute some kind of publicity; the great enemy is indifference. This attitude is to some extent vindicated by the way in which the public responded to works of art; it is noticeable how many late nineteenth- and twentieth-century works of lasting value were virtually ignored when they appeared, and how many that were instant successes have come to seem negligible.

It might be argued that serious writers and readers now come from roughly the same educational group, and are therefore likely to share certain presuppositions. The embattled antagonism between bourgeois readers and *déclassé* writers appears in this century to have evaporated in the face of common educational systems. But such presuppositions and beliefs as are shared have as their basis assumptions that are at least very limiting to allegory of the older kind. This is because, apart from the legacy of Romantic individualism, one of the more profound influences on the reading public has been psychology. Freudian psychology, and certainly Freudian psychology as commonly understood, offers a later, but perhaps more pervasive, sanctification of the needs and desires of the individual. Jungian theories, with their emphasis on the collective unconscious, could well offer more meat to the allegorist; but it is Freud rather than Jung who produced the theories that proved most influential.

It is interesting to observe the extent to which elements in Freudian psychology operate in ways similar to myth or allegory. As in myth, particular powers and functions are isolated and derived from constant sources; as in allegory, the operations and responses of an individual's mind are separated out into various components: Ego, Super-Ego, Id, Libido. In *Two Concepts of Allegory*, A. D. Nuttall quotes Husserl's comment that it is easy to transform 'a pure psychology of the inner life into a self-styled transcendental phenomenology' (p.17), and points to the similarities between 'Aphrodite breathed in me' and 'My Libido overcame me'. Freud posited rules according to which dream-events may be interpreted, suggesting that these events are attempts by the subconscious to reconcile unwelcome contradictions (exactly as Lévi-Strauss argues that the function of myth is to harmonize the contradictions between experience and unconscious desires). The allegorist also divides up the cosmos into separate principles and powers represented by personifications, and then creates an allegorical action in which these interact until some kind of harmony is reached either by conflict or progress. The appeal of post-Freudian psychology lies partly in its functional similarities to myth and allegory; it answers the needs for collectively acceptable explanation, simple, clearly systematized, and susceptible to being rendered in popularized forms.

But if both Romantic individualism and post-Freudian psychology offer what is in a sense an internalization of previous mythologies, theodicies, and ethical systems, that internalization is precisely what constitutes the greatest literary disadvantage. The external world is deprived of value except in so far as individual values may be projected on to it or derived from it. 'The Spirit of Nature was *upon me* there.' Correlatives of this are, first, the tentative and infrequent use of images that have traditional meanings established outside the work as well as within it; second, the reluctance of many critics to interpret and evaluate according to principles or evidence external to the work considered. Nor is the multiplication of journalistic forms in which the first-person observer/reporter is dominant, unconnected ('I, Norman Mailer, observing the launching of the first moon ship', rather than 'I, Poet and Dreamer, recording as Everyman for all men').

It is difficult to conceive of an allegory centred on events or persons with no significance in contexts outside the work. To personify Ymagynatyf, or Mammon, or Bel Acueil, is to assume that these qualities recognizable, interpretable, or even familiar to the reader; to describe single combat between two knights called Sansfoy and Redcrosse assumes that the rules of chivalric encounter are not entirely alien to the reader, and that the names alone carry some weight of meaning that provides a reason for the conflict. Even where we are not dealing with personified agents but with what Fletcher calls 'conceptual heroes' (Christian, Ahab) the subordination of character to thematic rather than psychological concerns entails constant analogy with other heroes and their actions.

Kafka is remarkable in having written allegories which discard these assumptions: both *The Castle* and *The Trial* and several of the short stories centre on the intensely restricted world of the individual. When K. sees the picture of the Judge in Titorelli's studio, and questions him as to the significance of the figure behind the sitter, the mythological allusions take on outstanding significance by virtue of their rarity. And even here the mythology is self-cancelling: the painter has been told to paint the figure of Justice, with scales and blindfolded eyes, but to combine it with the figure of Victory by adding wings to the heels. As K. points out, this is not a good combination, since 'Justice must stand quite still, or else the scales will waver and a just verdict will become impossible' (p.162). The figure sweeping into the foreground 'no longer suggested the goddess of Justice, or even the goddess of Victory, but looked exactly like a goddess of the Hunt in full cry' (p.163). The classical iconography cancels itself out, and the dominant significance of the figure is the significance that its appearance has for K.

The names of the various characters in *The Trial* are deliberately neutral, suggesting only professions or occupations, and even these suggestions are denied by the action; the Advocate is never seen pleading his client's case, the Examining Magistrate does not conduct a public examination, Titorelli the painter is never seen painting and his 'studio' turns out to be annexed to the Court. Both he and the Priest belong ultimately to the Court, the first as 'Court painter' and the second as 'prison chaplain'. K. himself, whose name instantly poses a problem of identity, though claiming to be 'the junior manager of a large Bank' is continually sent off on missions that prevent him practising this occupation. Even the hierarchy that is suggested by Magistrate, Judge, great Judge, is undercut by the continuous implications that these are in fact the lowest of the low and that there exists an infinity of superior officers, unknowable to the ignorant Accused. The same technique occurs in *The Castle*, where K. never acts as a Land-Surveyor, and where the ramifying chain of command among the officials of the Castle becomes less clear as the narrative proceeds.

The curiously inverted nature of Kafka's allegory is very clear in the scene in the Cathedral. In the arrangement made posthumously by Max Brod on the basis of hearing Kafka read and discuss his works, this scene is the penultimate chapter in *The Trial*, and immediately precedes K.'s execution. K., waiting for 'the Italian' who never turns up, inspects a huge altar-piece by the light of his pocket torch:

The first thing K. perceived, partly by guess, was a huge armoured knight on the outermost verge of the picture. He was leaning on his sword, which was stuck into the bare ground,

bare except for a stray blade of grass or two. He seemed to be
watching attentively some event unfolding itself before his
eyes. It was surprising that he should stand so still without
approaching nearer to it. Perhaps he had been set there to stand
guard. ... When he played the torch over the rest of the altar
piece he discovered that it was a portrayal of Christ being
laid in the tomb, quite conventional in style although a fairly
recent painting. (p.226)

No interpretation of the altar-piece is offered, and the reader is left
to guess whether the surprising stillness of the knight is analogous
to K.'s reluctance to exert himself in the establishing of his
innocence, and whether or not the tomb anticipates K.'s death. It
is in the Cathedral also that the priest tells K. the parable of the
man from the country, who waits all his life outside a door begging
to be admitted to the Law. At his death he suddenly realizes that
no-one else has ever passed through the door or waited outside it,
and he asks the doorkeeper why this is so. He is told that this door
was intended for him alone even though he has never entered it. In
the subtle and intelligent film version made by Orson Welles, this
story is used as a suitably enigmatic prologue and epilogue. In the
book, the enigma is deepened by the priest's various analyses. He
offers several interpretations, many of them contradictory, exactly
as if he were quoting the writings of legal authorities on a particular
case, or of medieval allegorical exegetes of the Bible: 'The com-
mentators note in this connexion ...', 'Some push this mode of
interpretation even further ...', 'Many aver that ...', 'The scriptures
are unalterable and the comments often enough merely express the
commentator's bewilderment ...'. De Lorris, Bunyan, Dante,
Spenser, Langland, and Swift all give their heroes the advice and
clarification of various Expositors and Guides. But for K. the
interpretations offered at various points in the action create confusion rather than diminishing it. (In *In the Penal Colony* the
workings of the machine that executes the convicted is expounded
by an admiring officer: finally he not only immolates himself on it,
but the machine itself breaks down wildly and horrifically.) K. is
precipitated back into his own individuality: there is no interpretation that has more validity than his own. What he makes of
his experiences has at least the virtue of cohesion, since it derives
from a single source. But even as the executioner's knife enters his

heart he is still asking questions, puzzling; his last gesture is to raise his hands with all the fingers spread out, a combination of supplication and a shrug of resignation. The world and his experience of it is incomprehensible. It might be fair to say that Kafka allegorized experiences which reflect precisely those social and cultural tendencies most inimical to allegorical writing of the earlier kind.

The qualitative changes in allegory and the ways in which critics have responded to it during the last century and the beginning of our own reflect the recurrent polarities of intellectual history. Given the dualistic aspect of the mode it is perhaps appropriate that its changing status and purposes mirror the major dichotomies of philosophy, politics, and literary theory: individualism versus collectivism, liberalism versus authoritarianism, pluralism versus monism, positivism versus idealism, existentialism versus structuralism, anarchy versus conservatism, originality versus convention, particularity versus generality, character versus theme, free-enterprise capitalism versus the total world view of ecological thinking. Our response to any allegory will be influenced by which side of these dichotomies elicits our sympathy. Recent fiction has tended to be organized by theme and intellectual patterning rather than by plot, and to treat characters symbolically rather than naturalistically – and comparable criteria to be applied in literary criticism. Political thinking and such disciplines as history, anthropology, and linguistics have been concerned with large underlying structures and movements rather than with individuals and individual texts. We may now have a more favourable climate for allegory, though it remains to be seen whether this is no more than a kind of revivalist speculation. We certainly have no metaphysical or moral absolutes of the kind that readily lent themselves as the basis of earlier allegories. It seems no accident that the most overtly, consciously, allegorical forms in the twentieth century are Science Fiction and children's books (and of course the cinema above all, which is regrettably beyond the scope of this book). In the case of the former, science, or popular scientism, offers opportunities for investing material events and the control of material events with moral significance. Scientists still talk of constructing 'a model' when verbalizing their findings; the well-educated scientist is perhaps the only person amongst us for whom a model of the universe has any connection with truth, even if he knows that model to be historically relative. The evil scientist in Science

Fiction is like Archimago in *The Faerie Queene* – he can control material reality to disadvantage his opponents, and is both agent and representative of the Hostile Power. The material and the immaterial can also be easily associated in children's literature, because children readily accept stories that move in that area where the imagination embodies abstractions, and abstracts from particulars. And children are often not harassed by a sense of finite, enclosed, individuality. Wordsworth commented bitterly on the way in which the exigencies of formal education work against the eclecticisms and coherence of imagination. The child knows about Geography, Science, and Morals, but as some more un-mediated thought, at once both more and less empirical, comes to him:

> Some intermeddler still is on the watch
> To drive him back, and pound him, like a stray,
> Within the pinfold of his own conceit.
> Meanwhile old grandame earth is grieved to find
> The playthings, which her love designed for him,
> Unthought of: in their woodland beds the flowers
> Weep and the river sides are all forlorn.
> Oh! give us once again the wishing cap
> Of Fortunatus, and the invisible coat
> Of Jack the Giant-Killer, Robin Hood,
> And Sabra in the forest with Saint George.
> The child, whose love is here, at least, doth reap
> One precious gain, that he forgets himself.
>   (*The Prelude*, v 334-46)

Bibliography

1 *Allegorical works*

ALAIN DE LILLE, *Anticlaudianus* and *De Planctu Naturae*. In J. P. Migne, *Patrologia Cursus Completus*, Series Latina, Vol. 210.
—— *The Plaint of Kind*, trans. D. M. Moffat, Yale Studies in English 36, Yale University Press, 1908.
BUNYAN, JOHN, *The Pilgrim's Progress*, ed. J. B. Wharey, 2nd edn revised by Roger Sharrock, Clarendon Press, Oxford, 1960.
CHAUCER, GEOFFREY, *The Works*, ed. F. N. Robinson, 2nd edn Oxford University Press, London, 1957.
DANTE, ALIGHIERI, *La Divina Commedia*, ed. Natalino Sapegno, Milan, 1957.
HOGG, JAMES, *The Private Memoirs and Confessions of a Justified Sinner*, with introduction by André Gide, The Cresset Press, London, 1947.
HUXLEY, ALDOUS, *Brave New World* (1932), Penguin, 1955.
KAFKA, FRANZ, *The Castle* (1926), trans. Willa and Edwin Muir, Penguin, 1957. (Page references to the 1968 reprint.)
—— *The Trial* (1925), trans. Willa and Edwin Muir, Penguin, 1953. (Page references to the 1970 reprint.)
LANGLAND, WILLIAM, *Piers Plowman*, B text ed. W. W. Skeat, Early English Text Society, original series no. 38, 1869.
—— *Piers the Ploughman*, trans. J. F. Goodridge, Penguin, 1959. (References to the 1960 reprint. Editions after 1966 cut the valuable introduction by half.)
LORRIS, GUILLAUME DE, AND MEUN, JEAN DE, *Le Roman de la Rose*, ed. E. Langlois, Société des Anciens Textes Français, Paris, 1914-24.
—— *The Romaunt of the Rose*, translation attributed to Chaucer, in *The Works*, ed. F. N. Robinson.
MELVILLE, HERMAN, *Moby Dick* (1851), ed. Harold Beaver, Penguin, 1972.
ORWELL, GEORGE, *Animal Farm* (1945), Penguin 1951.
—— *1984* (1949), Penguin, 1954.
PEAKE MERVYN, *Titus Groan* (1946), Penguin, 1968.
—— *Gormenghast* (1950), Penguin, 1969.
—— *Titus Alone* (1959), Penguin, 1970.
SHELLEY, MARY, *Frankenstein* (1818), ed. M. K. Joseph, Oxford University Press, London, 1969.

SPENSER, EDMUND, *The Poetical Works*, ed. J. C. Smith and E. De Selincourt, Oxford Standard Authors Series, Oxford University Press, London, 1912.

SWIFT, JONATHAN, *Gulliver's Travels* and *A Tale of a Tub*, in *Works*, ed. H. C. Davis, 1939-63. (See also the separate edn of *A Tale of a Tub*, ed. A. C. Guthkelch and D. Nichol Smith, Clarendon Press, Oxford, 1958.)

WOLLESTONECRAFT GODWIN, MARY, see 'Shelley, Mary'.

2 *Secondary material and criticism*

ALPERS, PAUL J. (ed.), *Edmund Spenser*, Penguin Critical Anthologies, Penguin, 1969.

AUERBACH, ERICH, *Mimesis*, trans. W. R. Trask, Anchor Books, New York, 1957.

—— 'Figura', in *Scenes from the Drama of European Literature*, Meridian, 1959.

COLERIDGE, SAMUEL TAYLOR, *Miscellaneous Criticism*, ed. T. M. Raysor, Cambridge, Massachusetts, 1936. (Some of Coleridge's comments on allegory and Spenser in particular reproduced in Alpers, *op. cit.*)

CURTIUS, ERNST ROBERT, *European Literature and the Latin Middle Ages*, trans. W. R. Trask, Bollingen Series XXXVI, New York, 1953.

EMPSOM, WILLIAM, *Some Versions of Pastoral*, Peregrine Books, Penguin, 1966.

FARAL, EDMOND (ed.), *Les Arts poétiques du XIIIe et du XIIIe siècle; recherches et documents sur la technique littéraire du moyen âge*, Paris, 1924.

FLETCHER, ANGUS, *Allegory: The Theory of a Symbolic Mode*, Cornell University Press, 1964.

FOWLER, ALASTAIR, 'Emblems of Temperance in *The Faerie Queene*, Book II', *Review of English Studies*, n.s. Vol. II, 1960.

FRANK, R. W., 'The Art of Reading Medieval Personification Allegory', *English Literary History* 20, 1953.

FRYE, NORTHROP, *Anatomy of Criticism*, Princeton, 1957.

GOMBRICH, E. H., *Meditations on a Hobby Horse*, Phaidon Press, London, 1963.

HONIG, EDWIN, *Dark Conceit: The Making of Allegory*, Oxford University Press, New York, 1966.

HORSTMANN, C. (ed.), *The Minor Poems of the Vernon MS*, Early English Text Society, orginal series 98, 117, 1892.

JOHNSON, SAMUEL, *Preface to Shakespeare*, in *Johnson on Shakespeare*, selected by Walter Raleigh, Oxford University Press, London, 1916.

JOSIPOVICI, GABRIEL, *The World and the Book*, Macmillan, London, 1971.

LEACH, EDMUND, *Lévi-Strauss*, Fontana Modern Masters Series, Fontana, London, 1970.

LEWIS, C. S., *The Allegory of Love*, Oxford University Press, London, 1936. (References to the corrected 1938 reprint.)

MARLOWE, CHRISTOPHER, *The Works*, ed. C. F. Tucker Brooke, Oxford University Press, 1910.

NUTTALL, A. D., *Two Concepts of Allegory*, Routledge & Kegan Paul, London, 1967.

OFFORD, M. Y. (ed.), *The Parlement of the Thre Ages*, Early English Text Society, No. 246, Oxford University Press, 1959.

ORWELL, GEORGE, *Inside the Whale and Other Essays* (1957), Penguin, 1962. (Reference to the 1968 reprint.)

OWST, G. R., *Literature and Pulpit in Medieval England: a neglected chapter in the history of English letters and of the English people*, Cambridge University Press, 1933.

PIEHLER, PAUL, *The Visionary Landscape, a Study in Medieval Allegory*, Edward Arnold, London, 1971.

PRUDENTIUS, *Psychomachia*, trans. H. J. Thompson, Loeb Classical Library, 1949.

PUTTENHAM, GEORGE, *The Arte of English Poesie*, ed. G. D. Willcock and A. Walker, Cambridge University Press, 1936.

SIDNEY, SIR PHILIP, *An Apology for Poetry, or, The Defence of Poesy*, ed. Geoffrey Shepherd, Medieval and Renaissance Library, Nelson, London, 1965.

SPEIRS, JOHN, '*Wynnere and Wastoure* and *The Parlement of the Thre Ages*', *Scrutiny* XVII, 1950.

STERNE, LAWRENCE, *The Life and Opinions of Tristram Shandy, Gentleman*, With an introduction by J. C. Powys, Macdonald, London, 1949.

TRAVERSI, D. A., 'Revaluations (x): The Vision of Piers Plowman', *Scrutiny* V, 1936, pp.276-91. (Revised reprint in *The Pelican Guide to English Literature*, Vol. I.)

TRESSELL, ROBERT, *The Ragged-Trousered Philanthropists* (1914), unabridged edition, Panther, London, 1972.

TUVE, ROSEMOND, *Allegorical Imagery*, Princeton University Press, 1966.

YATES, FRANCES A., *The Art of Memory* (1966), Peregrine Books, Penguin, 1969.

YEATS, W. B., *Selected Criticism*, ed. Norman Jeffares, Macmillan, London, 1964.